SHARKS
IN BRITISH SEAS

Second Edition

Richard Peirce

Published by:
Shark Cornwall, Dulverton House, Crooklets,
Bude, Cornwall, EX23 8NE.

First published: 2008
Second edition: 2011

ISBN no. 978-0-9558694-3-3

Editors : Anthony Bush, Tim Davison
Illustrator : Per Larsen
Photo credits/copyrights : As on photos
Front cover photograph : Chris Fallows

Printed and bound in England by
SR Print Management Limited, Watling Court, Orbital Plaza,
Cannock, Staffordshire. WS11 0EL

– – – – – –

**"This book is dedicated to the memory of Grant Bates,
a friend and mentor, and tireless campaigner seeking to ensure
a future for this threatened group of animals"**

– – – – – –

SOON TO BE PUBLISHED BY THE SAME AUTHOR.

"Shark Adventures – the Expeditions"
"Hanging Places in Devon & Cornwall"

OTHER PRODUCTS
Available online at www.sharkconsoc.com
"Sharks in British Seas" – DVD (Simon Spear – Richard Peirce)
"Shark Attack Britain" – DVD (Shark Bay Films)
"Shark Attack Britain" – Book (Shark Cornwall)
"Sharks off Cornwall & Devon" – Book (Tormark)
"Pirates of Devon & Cornwall" – Book (Shark Cornwall)

FOREWORD
Richard E Grant

'Cows are statistically more dangerous to Britons than sharks' is just one of the multitude of fascinating facts to be found in these pages. But there is nothing quite like a shark story to get your pulse soaring. It's extraordinary that, having been swimming the oceans for 400 millions years, sharks have been hunted down, fished and reduced to an endangered species within our lifetime, in less than a century.

Whatever the grim statistics, no other creatures, apart from crocodiles, seem to grip our imaginations quite like sharks do. Lions in Africa seem to have grown inured to busloads of camera clickers. Crocs mostly seem to lie around basking in the sun. But sharks are always on the move, ready to come and get you! In my experience, a shark story is a guaranteed attention grabber – making adult listeners as wide eyed as they once were when listening to Grimm's fairy tales - satisfying our deep-seated need to be terrified, by the unseen, the unknown and the untamed.

Unlike many endangered species, these creatures don't have any cuddly, 'adopt a Great White' cosiness about them. This book seeks to present the facts alongside the fictions that have accrued into myth and legend about these 'blank eyed', apparently unknowable animals.

When I was eight-years-old on holiday in Mozambique, our motorboat engine conked out whilst we were cruising around a large lagoon. I will never forget the sight of a shark's fin breaking the surface and heading towards us. My father tried to keep us all calm, that is until the shark circled the boat and then repeatedly 'bumped' into it, rocking it from side to side. We all started screaming. Because the water was so calm and flat, our yelling was heard some distance away and another launch eventually came to our rescue.

It turned out that the Zambezi shark had been 'trapped' within the lagoon for six months when the mouth into the open sea had sanded up during high tides and, reportedly, became increasingly aggressive. This experience inspired my lifelong fascination with sharks. In retrospect, I assume the 'bumping' of our boat was simply the shark's curiosity rather than any "Spielbergian" mission to sushi us all for its supper.

When I was offered the chance to join Ruby Wax, Colin Jackson and Amy Nuttall inside a perspex 'drum' off the coast of Cape Town to see Great Whites under water and close up, I dived at it. NOTHING prepared me for the sheer exhilaration and adrenalin rush of being within 'touching' distance of these powerful animals.

The facts about sharks outstrip their fiction. If we cut shark fin soup off the menu (rather than their backs) we could increase and restore shark populations to what they once were. What say you?

Richard E Grant.

INTRODUCTION

In 2003 I wanted to buy a book on British sharks to give as a present to my friend Craig Ferreira from South Africa, who had come to work with me on an expedition off Cornwall. I couldn't find a book in print so Craig missed out on his gift.

When chumming (laying a scent trail in the water) most of the time is spent doing very little while waiting for sharks to turn up, so there's lots of time to think and hatch plots on these expeditions. Whilst chumming in the Adriatic in 2005 my thoughts kept returning to the irony of my travelling around all over the world seeking sharks, when we have some 30 species in British waters. Many become aware of the existence of sharks in our seas only when screaming tabloid headlines give them a totally erroneous impression of these amazing and beautiful creatures.

I realised that clearly there was a job to be done, and decided to make it my mission to bring the existence of our sharks to the widest possible audience. Also, I wanted to ensure that my audience realised that man is the threat to sharks and not the other way round.

My trying to find a book to give Craig had told me there wasn't one, so I realised there was a gap to fill, and filling it would fit in with my mission. We've now started shark cage diving in Britain, generated a large number of sensible headlines, deployed the first satellite tags on Porbeagle Sharks, and secured the first underwater Porbeagle images. Also, I've presented a Radio 4 shark series, and we've started to make films about British sharks - so the mission is well underway.

Researching and writing the first edition of 'Sharks in British Seas' taught me how little I knew about our sharks, and doing the revisions and updates, and adding the extra material in this second edition has continued my learning process. In addition to revisions and updates this second edition has a new comment from Sir David Jason, a greatly expanded shark attack chapter, three new chapters, and many new photographs and illustrations. I hope you enjoy reading the book as much as I've enjoyed putting it together.

Richard Peirce.

SHARKS
IN BRITISH SEAS

Comment from Sir David Jason

Foreword by Richard E Grant

Introduction by Richard Peirce

Illustrations – Photographs, maps, diagrams and cartoons

SECTION 1.

SECTION 2.

Chapter One

THE WORLD OF SHARKS

Shark. There are few words that send a shiver down the spine so successfully. Peter Benchley's book Jaws, later made into a blockbuster film by Steven Spielberg, identified man's fears and played on them. The fear of being eaten alive, the fear of being outside your element and the fear of the unknown are all exploited menacingly in the early minutes of the film, when the first victim falls prey to attack. What can be more chilling than swimming on the surface of the ocean wondering what unseen dangers are lurking beneath you? This is the stuff of nightmares and truly terrifying.

Man has feared and demonised sharks since the earliest times. Many cultures with strong ties to the sea feature sharks prominently in their art and mythology. In the Cook and Solomon islands, sharks are worshipped; they appear in Australian aboriginal mythology; sharks play a central part in many Polynesian legends; and Hawaiians and Tahitians believe dead relatives can return in the form of sharks. In the Mediterranean, sharks also feature from early times in both Roman and ancient Greek literature. In the fifth century BC, Herodotus related how shipwrecked Persian sailors were eaten by sharks, and around 330 BC, Aristotle wrote in detail about sharks in his Historia Animalium, accurately describing the difference between them and bony fish.

By the start of the 20th century, sharks were firmly established as fearsome and loathsome predators. Shipwreck incidents in both world wars reconfirmed this outlook. When the USS Indianapolis was sunk in the Far East at the end of World War II, 900 men went into the water, but only 317 survived the sharks and the elements. Thereafter, the shark's position as a hate figure equalled that of any monster before or since.

There are at least 456 shark species in the world's oceans and around 30 can be found in British seas. Of the United Kingdom's shark species only the Mako, the Blue, the Thresher and the Porbeagle are recorded as being dangerous to man. However, with these species being depleted by more than 60 per cent due to overfishing, having the chance to see such magnificent animals must be regarded as a privilege, not something to provoke fear and media hysteria. Many will be surprised to learn that – in addition to Makos, Blues, Threshers, and Porbeagles – Hammerheads, Soupfin Sharks (Tope), Greenland Sharks, Sixgill and Sevengill Sharks are also on the 'British list'.

Fish are split into two main groups: Teleosts, which have bony skeletons and Chondrichthyes, which have skeletons made of cartilage. Sharks belong to the group Chondrichthyes or cartilaginous (non-bony) fishes. Chondrichthyan fishes are divided into two sub-groups: the Elasmobranchii and the Holocephali. Sharks are part of the former and there are eight Orders of sharks (see Section 2).

Sharks are superbly adapted to their environment. Light pliable cartilage instead of heavy dense bones, together with their highly streamlined shapes, promotes efficient movement. Our warm-blooded sharks such as the Mako, Thresher and Porbeagle often rely on speed to catch their prey. Others such as the Angelsharks are ambush predators and depend on their camouflage to conceal them from their prey.

Sharks possess the same five senses as humans – smell, taste, touch, hearing and sight – although, in some instances, they work relatively better in their world than ours do in our environment. Experiments with Lemon and Nurse Sharks have established their olfactory ability to detect concentrations as low as one part per million. When working with Blue Sharks off North Cornwall, I lay 'chum' in the water. This is essentially a scent trail made of mashed up oily fish such as mackerel. (Incidentally, the English name for chum is rubby dubby). I very often have to wait several hours for Blue Sharks to find us. This not only illustrates their relative scarcity, but also indicates that, for our trail to be effective, we have to wait for it to cover several miles. When sharks have picked up the smell, they will swim up the trail looking for a meal. The concentration of chum materials in the water two or three miles from the boat is minute but the sharks still find us, thereby confirming their acute sense of smell.

In addition to the five senses they share with us, sharks also have two extra senses: the lateral line, a mechanosensory system, and the ampullae of Lorenzini, an electrosensory system.

The lateral line extends from the head to the base of the tail (caudal) fin, and consists of a pair of tubes containing sets of sensory cells with protrusions known as neuromasts or hair cells. The hairs react to movement and changes in pressure. Working in conjunction with the lateral line are the pit organs, which are pockets scattered around the body that also contain sensory cells. These systems enable sharks to detect changes in pressure, tiny vibrations and water displacements, and to determine the direction from which they are coming.

The ampullae of Lorenzini make up an electrosensory system used to detect weak electrical fields. Elongated, jelly-filled tubes connect pores on the skin's surface to the ampullae, which contain receptor cells. These pores are clearly visible as dark dots below the snout and behind the eyes. I have many times seen Great White Sharks apparently attracted to, and investigating, metal items such as propellers and shark cages. This is quite possibly due to the objects' electrical fields. It is believed that Hammerheads use a combination of their electrosensory and mechanosensory systems to detect prey buried in sand.

Sharks are carnivores with diets ranging from plankton to mammals, other sharks, large and small bony fish and invertebrates, including crustaceans. The dental array of sharks reflects this diet. The filter feeders (plankton eaters) have only tiny vestigial teeth, whereas the Great White has a formidable set of sharp triangular teeth perfectly suited to removing large chunks of flesh from their prey. The Mako has sharp, pointed, blade-like teeth ideal for tearing and trapping prey. Ocean bottom-dwelling sharks, which have crustaceans on their menu, have specialised teeth for crushing shells. A shark's mouth is a tooth factory, with new teeth being continuously formed in the gums inside the mouth and then moving outwards. The older teeth drop off making space for the new, which may last for anything from a month to a year.

Sharks breathe by extracting oxygen from the water as it passes over their gills. Water enters through the mouth, passes through the internal gill openings and is then expelled through the external gill outlet. There is less oxygen in water than in air, so sharks need to ensure a good, continual flow through their gills. Some species achieve this by using a system called 'ram ventilation', which forces water through the gills as the shark swims. Others rely on a combination of ram ventilation and a gill pump and often spend time motionless – either resting or sleeping on the sea floor – while the pump provides the flow of oxygenated water over their gills.

Assessing shark intelligence is extremely difficult but two things are known. Firstly, compared to many in the animal kingdom, sharks have large brains (and, as we have seen, they have two extra senses). Secondly, research carried out with Lemon and Nurse Sharks has shown that they can learn to perform actions, respond to stimuli and have memories.

In November 2003, a Great White Shark off the coast of South Africa in False Bay was fitted with a pop-off satellite tag that detached 6,897 miles away off Exmouth in Western Australia. The journey had taken 99 days and, for a large percentage of the time, the shark, a female, had been close to the surface. It is clear that she travelled a direct route and this suggests she possessed the ability to navigate, possibly using stellar clues. This was reinforced when she was recognised six months later back in False Bay. What had caused her to leave a well supplied feeding area and make her transoceanic journey? Her direct line travel there and back indicates she was on a mission, which she achieved before swimming home. (N.B. This shark was subsequently nicknamed Nicole after the actress Nicole Kidman).

－－－－－

Mention shark behaviour to most people and it's more than likely that they will conjure up an image of aggression: attacks, feeding frenzies and threatening fins slicing through the water signalling a prelude to a strike. While it is true that most sharks spend much of their time hunting and eating, most feeding frenzies are man-induced, and attacks on humans are extremely rare. Typically, there are fewer than ten human deaths attributable to shark attacks in the whole world in a year. Recently, the number of reported shark-related deaths has been five or six a year although tragically this figure climbed to 14 in 2011. There are less not more sharks in the oceans, and there is nothing to indicate that shark behaviour is changing. What is changing however is human behaviour in that increased human leisure use of the water means more people spending more time in our seas each year. This gives rise to increased opportunities for interaction between sharks and humans, and sometimes with tragic results. Bees, hippos, cars, alcohol, sex, over-exercise, under-exercise, snakes, earthquakes and almost anything else you can think of are more dangerous to man than sharks.

Sharks don't form family groups as such but some species do school or aggregate. The Scalloped Hammerhead is well known for this behaviour and, in British waters, the Porbeagle does the same, making it very vulnerable to targeted fishing. The Spurdog (aka the Piked Dogfish or Spiny Dogfish) will also form aggregations. When schools or aggregations are created there will probably be social interactions but there has been very little research in this area. At certain times of the year Porbeagles aggregate by sex and this, in addition to the ease with which longline fishing boats can catch them, increases their vulnerability. Cooperative hunting has been observed in some species such as the Sevengill Shark and there is anecdotal evidence of this activity involving Great Whites, Porbeagles, Threshers, Oceanic Whitetips, Sand Tigers and some reef sharks.

The popular perception is that mammals are warm-blooded and fish cold-blooded. However, some sharks including the Great White, Porbeagle, Mako and Thresher maintain a body temperature of a constant level above that of the surrounding water. This is achieved through a heat exchange system known as the 'rete mirabile' or 'marvellous net', which is a network of tiny capillaries. Cold oxygenated blood from the gills runs parallel but in the opposite direction to deoxygenated blood warmed by muscle action returning to the gills. These vessels running alongside each other exchange heat highly effectively, with no heat loss to the sea.

Most sharks possess a tough and durable skin that man has turned into various leather articles and which has also been used as sandpaper. Embedded in a shark's skin are small, sharp, teeth-like scales known as dermal denticles, which fall out but are replaced continuously during life. As well as providing physical protection, dermal denticles create a surface that has virtually no surface drag. Top swimmers wearing Speedo bodysuits to eliminate drag are emulating this shark characteristic.

The largest shark, which is also the largest fish in the sea, is the Whale Shark, known to reach lengths of up to 15 metres (46 feet). At the other end of the scale, the tiny Pigmy Shark measures just 15 centimetres (six inches). Neither of these is found in our waters – our sharks range from the giant Basking Shark, the second largest fish in the world achieving lengths of over 10 metres (30 feet), down to the Velvet Belly measuring 60 centimetres (two feet). Along the way, there is the 5.5 metre plus (18 feet) Greenland Shark, the Sharpnose Sevengill, the Bluntnose Sixgill, the Kitefin Shark (aka Dark Charlie), the Bramble Shark, the Angelshark and many others, including the more widely recognised Hammerheads, Makos, Threshers, Porbeagles and Blues.

Britain's shores are washed by the North Sea, Irish Sea, Celtic Sea, English Channel, the Bristol Channel, the sea of the Hebrides, and the Atlantic Ocean. Together, they provide a huge diversity of marine environments that can support abundant populations of sharks. Sadly though, despite these riches, the extinction clock is ticking for many of our species due to over-exploitation by man. Britain has led the world in many initiatives, and in recent years has started to play a leading role in protecting not just the sharks in our waters but those around the world.

The earliest sharks appeared on the planet some 400 million years ago. There is something unbalanced – indeed almost criminal – in the thought that the recently-arrived species called mankind should be responsible for threatening the extinction of sharks. The main reason the extinction clock is ticking so close to midnight is the overfishing of sharks to satisfy the demand from the Far East for fins for soup. The rapid economic development of the Chinese and other Far Eastern economies has brought luxuries within reach of an ever-increasing consumer market. Sharks really are in the soup, bowls of this expensive dull-tasting delicacy being largely responsible for pushing one of earth's oldest inhabitants to the verge of extinction.

Chapter Two

THE GREAT WHITE ENIGMA

Why isn't the Great White Shark a permanent resident in British waters?

Conditions are broadly similar to those where large resident populations flourish, such as South Africa, southern Australia, and California. The nearest confirmed Great White Shark to our waters was a female captured in 1977 in the northern Bay of Biscay off La Rochelle – 168 nautical miles from Land's End . In 2003/04 the female Great White nicknamed Nicole completed a six-month, 13,000+ mile journey from False Bay in South Africa to Western Australia, where she turned around and then swam back to South Africa. So, clearly, 168 miles is no distance for these sharks.

Fishermen's stories are renowned for their colour and exaggeration. By the mid 1990's, I realised that I was continually hearing stories of large, powerful, unidentified sharks in UK waters. Could some of them be Great Whites? There was no reason why not, so I started logging each report.

My record keeping has not included all the reports I have received, because some claimed sightings were so ludicrous they weren't worth noting or considering further. However, from 1996 until the time of writing I can certainly say that I have heard of nearly 90 possible Great White Shark encounters. Of those, nine that I have investigated remain credible after further examination. I am not saying that these nine incidents involved Great Whites, but the descriptions given certainly fit those of Great White Sharks.

So do these sharks visit our shores or not? The jury is out and will remain so until firm proof exists – a carcass, tooth, tissue sample, photograph or some other conclusive evidence. However I believe there is a high probability that the creatures involved in some of the following incidents were indeed Great White Sharks.

The following report is an extract from a soon to be published book called 'The Shark Fisherman' by David Turner and is reproduced by kind permission of Little Egret Press and David Turner.

THE FALMOUTH GREAT WHITE: SUMMER 1965

"Of all the stories told of big sharks caught off Falmouth none was more intriguing than the following which was often discussed among shark anglers fishing out of Falmouth and beyond.

I wasn't on board on the day of the incident. It was 1965 the year before I fished out of Falmouth, a pity I didn't see it as I could have identified it easily, but in the following years I got to know several of the experienced anglers who were on board including Doug Phillips who hooked it, and skipper Robin Vinnicombe who came very close to boating it. The first I heard of it was in a tackle shop owned by Fred Taylor a respected Oxford angler. There was another lad in there about my age and he asked if I went shark fishing, I answered in the affirmative. He told me he and his dad spent their summer holidays sharking on board Eddie Lakeman's boat 'Penare' out of Mevagissey. They had just returned from their annual holiday the previous weekend, and he showed me a photograph of a 40lb Blue he had caught. There were large teeth marks on it. "As I was winding it in a big Mako grabbed it. There was also another big Mako hooked off Falmouth last week too, did you hear about that, it was hooked on Robin Vinnicombe's boat Inter Nos", he concluded. I hadn't heard about it but sure enough, when my copy of Angling Times arrived there was a report of 'an 800lb Mako' hooked and lost off Falmouth.

Maybe the attack on the hooked shark off Mevagissey and another incident were coincidental, but they suggested the presence of an unusually large shark in the waters off Cornwall in that summer of 1965. Businessman Harry Dutfield, director of a carpet manufacturing company and a keen shark fisherman had his own boat moored at Falmouth, he was a good friend of Robin and they often talked over the radio whilst out fishing. A couple of days before Doug Phillips hooked his shark, Harry was fishing off the Manacles. For a rubby dubby container Harry used a plastic laundry basket which was hanging over the side of his boat. Robin later relayed the following incident to me. "We were out a couple of days before Doug hooked his shark when Harry Dutfield came over the radio in an excited, almost hysterical voice, Inter Nos, Inter Nos, Harry here Rob, a bloody great shark has just come up and eaten the bloody rubby dubby basket", "Harry is not one to get overexcited", Robin said, "but he was that day alright, I'd never heard him like that before".

Although I was not there, I got the following account direct from Doug and Robin, confirmed by Frank Crooks and others also on board that day. After Harry Dutfields encounter with the large shark anticipation was probably heightened a couple of days later when Doug Phillips reel gave a couple of clicks on the ratchet. A light take is often the characteristic of a large shark, one of the few credible moments in the film "Jaws" is when the reel emits a couple of clicks and Quint picks up the rod without the others even noticing it, frequently that is the only indication given on the initial contact with a big fish. Doug waited for the reel to sound again and then reeled the line tight and struck. The hook went home and he told me he could feel it was a big fish right away but surprisingly it came quickly and easily to the boat.

To everyone's amazement within minutes the shark was alongside the boat. Those on board couldn't believe their eyes, even Robin, no stranger to big Makos, was stunned by its size. He later described it to me as being between twelve and fourteen feet long. Maybe he could have gaffed it then, but Robin was no fool and he knew that a fish of that size still had plenty of strength in it, and to try and boat it whilst still fresh would spell trouble, so instead he poked it in the eye with the gaff handle and it took off. Spray soaked most of those on board as line screamed from Doug's reel. Rob fired up' Inter Nos' and started to follow the monster shark.

For the next three hours the shark didn't show itself again, every time Doug regained line, the shark took it back and he was showing signs of fatigue when the shark re-surfaced, but it was still not over. For the next hour and a half the monster fish circled the boat on the surface and often just beyond the reach of the gaffs, which were all set to deal with it. All on board saw and watched it during this time but then – disaster! The line went slack, the 250lb braided stainless steel trace had frayed through on the sharks teeth, and it swam off into the deep leaving many intriguing questions behind. There is little doubt that a very large shark was hooked that day, it was clearly witnessed by around ten people and it doesn't seem credible that, collectively, they would fabricate and maintain such a story independent of each other for years to come. It was originally reported in the angling press as an "800lb Mako" and in occasional conversation merely as "the big shark" and the talk was of the epic battle rather than its unusual size. It was during a conversation some time later with Robin that he told me that the shark was between 12 & 14ft long. My immediate reaction was "Are you sure it wasn't a Great White". He admitted that he had a suspicion that it may have been, but he reported it as a Mako because he didn't think anyone would believe him, and he would become the laughingstock of the fleet without firm evidence.

What was the evidence? The shark was 'Mako shaped', short fins, stocky build, more or less symmetrical tail. To my knowledge no Porbeagle has ever been recorded anywhere near this size so that would narrow the possibilities down to a Mako or a Great White. A Mako is a possibility but further evidence tends to lean towards the shark having been a Great White. Although the shark was clearly visible for more than an hour, including a short period right alongside the boat, no-one saw the definitive evidence of the teeth, but the fact that the steel trace was frayed through suggests the teeth were serrated, the Mako has smooth curved needle shaped teeth unlikely to be capable of causing fraying of a steel trace. The final piece of evidence pointing towards a Great White, although again not conclusive, is the way the shark behaved on the line. When hooked, Makos, in by far the majority of cases, leap out of the water, in fact I only know of one caught off Cornwall that didn't jump out of the water and I caught it! This shark fought stubbornly and deep for much of the battle but there were none of the high speed runs associated with a Mako, especially one of this size!!

LOOE, CORNWALL: JULY 1970

John Reynolds, a Looe-based shark angling skipper, had been at sea all day about eight miles offshore with baited lines out and two rubby dubby bags dangling in the water. In that year Porbeagle and Blue Shark numbers were much higher than they are now, so it was unusual that they had not seen one all day. John's theory is that the lack of other sharks might have indicated the presence of a larger predator.

At sometime around 3pm John started to take in his lines and rubby dubby bags in preparation for returning to shore. He was pulling in the stern bag when a large shark appeared only a few feet behind the boat.

The animal looked straight at John, staying in a head-up position for some seconds before slipping back into the water and disappearing. John saw only the head but his description fits a Great White Shark and it is the only shark commonly known to spy-hop, which is the action of putting its head out of the water. Spy-hopping has rarely been observed in non-baited conditions and may not be natural behaviour. Current opinion suggests it is a response to concentrated scent stimuli at the surface like chum lines, and not an attempt to espy objects above the surface as had been previously thought. Spy-hopping (See page 19) is also practised by some whales but I have never heard of any of our existing shark species doing this.

The incident described by John fits a Great White Shark spy-hopping.

ST IVES, CORNWALL: AUGUST 1995

The following account was written by Sally Houseago who is convinced that she had a close encounter with a Great White Shark.

"I am credible and not some loony idiot. I have a degree in marine biology and I studied reef ecology in Tanzania. I am a fully qualified diver with the British Sub Aqua Club, and have dived over most of the world for research purposes. I have a keen interest in sharks and have done various work on reef sharks in coastal waters.

I was camping in St. Ives about 15 yrs ago, I was with friends and we decided to go out on the jet skis just outside the harbour which are available for public rent. The weather was dull and overcast and the water was reflecting this - the visibility was poor, but none of us minded. I was around 25 yrs old at the time and I recall this day vividly. I swapped with my friend from a sit down ski to a stand/kneel ski as I was more confident and enjoyed the speed. During the swap I felt as if there was something circling the 3 of us in the water as we exchanged. I was eventually left alone after my friends had clambered on the 2-seater which I held steady. As they pulled away I had a sense of panic and drew my legs up to my knees, I can't explain why. I could see nothing but I felt something was not right, as I did so a long dark shape torpedoed where my feet had just been. About 9 feet behind where I was it broke the surface with a huge splash and circled back. It was steel dark grey, with a white underside, the dorsal fin broke the surface and a Great White – young, about 10-12 feet long turned back towards me. I think it may have been male but I couldn't be sure as it was so quick. My friends did not see or hear as they had roared off, and I had to turn and swim to the jet-ski which had floated a small distance away. The shark and I both swam towards the ski, the shark went under the ski. I was terrified and got it running and pulled away, the shark swam almost underneath me for about 20ft, then disappeared.

I was fascinated, but not seeing it was more terrifying than seeing it and knowing where it was. We had a child in our group and I waved to get him off the jet-ski and on the boat. They thought I was having fun and waved back. In my concern I fell off, I never saw or felt the shark again and as our time was nearly up, I got back on and went over to my friends. I told the jet-ski guy who offered me a free hour which I did not accept. He told me it was probably a rare sunfish, I explained I knew what I had seen, it had been terrifying and fascinating at the same time. I explained I was an experienced fishing person, I also explained I had been on the Prince Madog research vessel, and I knew that was no sunfish. My friends thought I could have been mistaken. When we got to shore I tried to report the incident to the harbour master, but again no-one took it seriously. A few weeks after there was a shark incident and there was speculation about a Great White. I think it was Padstow. What had surprised me was the incident reflected how controlled, patient, and curious the shark had been. I felt it had circled us for a long time and had waited until I was on my own, it was an opportunistic attack, by an inexperienced predator. Had it been older and wiser I don't think I would be here now. I have not discussed it much since then, as no-one took it seriously, but I believe there may be Great Whites around our southern coasts. It was not a Mako, the head was more rounded and not so pointy."

Sally Houseago, Diss, Norfolk.

PADSTOW, NORTH CORNWALL: AUGUST 1999

A leaked tip-off to the national press about the sighting of a large shark thought to be a Great White up the coast from Padstow near Crackington Haven resulted in a hysterical reaction and, at times, insulting scepticism. This combination made the fishing party involved dismayed that the story ever got out.

Mike Turner and Phil Britts, who were aboard the Blue Fox together with Phil's wife, Rhona, and others all saw a large shark about 37 metres (40 yards) away. The dorsal fin was clearly visible approaching them in a straight line as they were releasing a Soupfin Shark (Tope) which they had caught earlier.

The shark, estimated to be 4.6 metres (15 feet) long, passed the stern and rolled, revealing a clear white underside separated from the grey/brown topside by a jagged line. It was visible for about a minute, having, at its nearest, come within 2 metres of the boat. Those on board believed that it had probably taken the Soupfin Shark (Tope) before disappearing.

A large black eye was noted and this, together with the colours and morphology described, are consistent with a Great White Shark. Mike had seen many Great Whites in South Africa and is adamant about the precision of his sighting. The others on board had seen a number of Porbeagles and Basking Sharks and ruled

Great White spotted in resort waters

August 2007. Hoax photo on the front page of the Newquay Guardian.

14

those out. It is noted that the proactive behaviour displayed in approaching the boat also fits the actions of a Great White Shark.

CAMBEAK HEAD, NORTH CORNWALL: AUGUST 1999

The Blue Fox incident took place off Cambeak Head, and the following day there was a similar occurrence in exactly the same location. Paul Vincent was out with his friend Jason Coe fishing for Soupfin Shark (Tope) from his 5.2 metre (17 foot) dory, Blissful. Paul had hooked a Soupfin Shark (Tope), and was about to lift it aboard using his gaff hook when a very large shark appeared and bit off the bottom two thirds of the captured shark before swimming off. Paul estimates that it was at least as long as his boat. His full description was a match for the shark seen by those aboard the Blue Fox: the same grey/brown dorsal side, white ventral side, large triangular dorsal fin, black eye and unhurried, investigative behaviour.

TINTAGEL HEAD, NORTH CORNWALL: SEPTEMBER 1999

Less than two weeks after these incidents and about 12 miles away near Tintagel Head, a lobster fisherman found a very large shark tangled up in his rope. He asked to remain anonymous — although his identity is known to me — and the whole incident I am about to describe was witnessed. When hauling in his pots there was what he thought was a snag in the line. It freed itself and then something hit the back of the davit. He went to look and saw the tail fin of a shark about 4.6 metres (15 feet) long. Because of its size, he thought it must be a Basking Shark.

Sharks cannot swim backwards and, if they land up in a rope, they often twist and become thoroughly entangled. Death follows unless they are freed quickly. And, unfortunately, that was the fate of this creature. As it had no commercial value, the only thing to do was to cut it loose. It was seen to have a slate grey topside and, as it was freed, it rolled showing a pure white underside. It also had what was described as a crescent-shaped mouth and triangular teeth. Basking Sharks and Porbeagles were both familiar to those on board and they were sure it was neither of those. At 4.6 metres (15 feet) what else could it have been? A Blue Shark or a Porbeagle? Very unlikely. A Mako? Again unlikely, and the colours and teeth as described don't fit.

So, three sharks each estimated to be the same size, each broadly fitting the same description and their sightings separated by only three weeks and 12 miles.

Coincidence? Same shark? A Great White Shark?

July 2007
Sound of Harris

July 2005
North Uist

December 2003
North East
Scotland

July 2003
Near
Ullapool

North Cornwall
August 1999
September 1999
July 2002
August 1995

July 1970
Looe

1965
Falmouth

The incidents that remain credible following investigation are clustered in two areas of the British Isles

Great White Shark spy-hopping. © Richard Peirce

This is what John Reynolds saw. © Richard Peirce

QUIES ISLANDS, NORTH CORNWALL: JULY 2002

On a clear, almost windless day Brian Bate was laying his lobster pots to the northeast of the Quies Islands, when, suddenly, a large fish between 3.6 metres (12 feet) and 4.6 metres (15 feet) in length leapt completely out of the water with something in its mouth. Brian went to the spot and found a large spreading pool of blood with pieces of seal blubber floating in it. Seagulls were already feeding on the smaller pieces of blubber.

Leaping out of the water is called breaching and what Brian saw was a typical breaching attack, the size, body shape and colours precisely fitting a Great White Shark. When I showed him various photographs of breaching sharks, including those of Makos and Threshers, he identified the Great White.

I suggested to him that it was a pity he hadn't retrieved one of the larger pieces of blubber in case a tooth might have been lodged in it, or the bite mark could have been identified. He told me that he didn't have a boathook and no sane person who had seen what he had would have started putting their hands in the water fishing around for bits of blubber!

If it wasn't a Great White, what else could it have been? For various reasons based on Brian's description, Blues, Porbeagles and Makos can be ruled out, which leaves a Killer Whale (Orca) as the only other possibility. Brian had seen many Orcas and was quite sure this hadn't been an Orca.

The triangular teeth of a Great White Shark and the sawing action of the jaws make dismemberment a typical occurrence, while this does not happen with the other sharks mentioned.

Two days after Brian Bate saw his 'breaching shark' kill a seal, a lone yachtsman sailed up the coast from Newquay to Padstow. He later recounted how a large shark followed in his wake for the greater part of his journey, and how he had sailed through the same water where Brian had seen the breaching attack. He is familiar with Basking Shark fins and is certain the shark that followed him was not one of those.

I went chumming in the Quies area with Brian two weeks after the seal predation and there were no seals to be seen where, normally, there is a small colony of between 15 and 20. The general area around Trevose Head, the Quies, the Camel Estuary and the offshore islands is home to several small population pockets of seals, but they did not return to the area until early October. I was alerted to two cases of washed-up seal remains, one in July before the Bates incident and the other in early August. Both carcasses consisted of only partial remains and both were extensively bird-pecked, making it impossible to determine how the seals died or learn anything from the wounds.

WESTERN ISLES, SCOTLAND: JULY 2003

To most people the idea of finding a Great White in Scottish waters would be no less improbable than finding the Loch Ness monster. Dr Simon Greenstreet was diving near Ullapool at the western edge of the Summer Isles, near Black Rock, on 4 July 2003. With him were his wife Wendy and two other divers in a 5.2 metre (17 foot) rigid inflatable boat. The Greenstreets had just finished their dive and the next pair were kitting up when a large fin was spotted some 28-36 metres (30–40 yards) away. The obvious thought was that it was a Basking Shark.

With the opportunity of swimming with a harmless shark in mind, Dr Greenstreet moved the boat closer. As soon as the engine started, the shark changed course and moved purposefully towards the boat. At this point, those on board still assumed it was a Basking Shark but, although nothing was said, doubts were creeping in.

When it was only 14 metres (15 yards) from the boat, the bulk of the shark was apparent. The distance from dorsal to tail fin was estimated at nearly three metres (9 feet). At that stage, the boat party realised this was no Basking Shark but it continued its approach, eventually swimming alongside only about half a metre away.

Those aboard judged the shark to be more than 4.6 metres (15 feet) in length. Dr Greenstreet has no specific shark interests but has seen enough Basking Sharks to know their particular characteristics. Unlike a Basking Shark, this one had a clearly defined white ventral side, a large solid broad-based triangular dorsal fin, a light grey dorsal side with clearly defined worn patches and smaller gills than the very large distinctive ones on a Basking Shark.

The description fits that of a Great White, as does its proactive behaviour in coming towards the boat when the engine was started. I believe that Dr Greenstreet and his party saw a Great White Shark.

NORTH EAST SCOTLAND: DECEMBER 2003

Five months after Dr Greenstreet's experience near Ullapool, a fisherman working off North East Scotland caught a large shark in his net. He did not wish to be named but I have interviewed him and others corroborate his story. What they all described was a large shark, 5.5 - 5.8 metres (18 - 19 feet) long with a large triangular dorsal fin snapping at small fish while it was trapped in the net. Teeth were observed but there is no accurate description of them, and the gills were not seen in sharp enough detail to be definitive. The fisherman was trying to work out how to release the shark when it managed to free itself.

The fisherman is not saying this was a Great White Shark, but he is adamant that it was not a Basking Shark. This does not leave many options and, as I had a photograph, I decided to send it to colleagues and seek their opinions. The image went to Great White Shark experts Ian Fergusson, Craig Ferreira, Jeremy Stafford-Deitsch, Leonard Compagno, Rolf Cyabaiski and others. Ian Fergusson and Leonard Compagno, two of the world's leading experts, collaborated in their reply and shared the opinion that, had I not told them the location was Scotland, but instead had said South Africa, southern Australia, or California, their first choice of identity would have been a Great White. However, because I had said "Scotland", they started thinking what else it might have been.

This is interesting. If I had simply said "I think this is a Great White; what do you think?", there is a good chance that two globally-renowned shark experts would have stuck to their original identification and the photograph would now be the first likely proof of a Great White in British waters.

NORTH UIST, SCOTLAND: JULY 2005

Modern languages school teacher Philip Harding, his colleague Alan and Alan's two teenage children were trolling for Pollock two miles south of Locheport at Aignish Point on the east coast of North Uist when Philip cut the engine to set up rods. At this point, a very large shark came up vertically beside the boat and had a good look at those on board before slowly diving and disappearing.

The features noticed were:
- a dark grey/bronzy dorsal side
- a pure white ventral side, so white that, for a split second, Philip thought the creature was an Orca before realising that it was a shark
- the shark was the length of the boat – 4.9 metres (16 feet)
- a very large girth and a solid (non-floppy), pointed, triangular dorsal fin

Philip and Alan are both very familiar with Basking Sharks and are quite adamant this was not one of those. However, the next day, just to be sure, Philip went to look at a freshly-dead Basking Shark caught in a net off Lochmaddy. Thereafter, he was able to confirm his initial impression that the morphology of the two sharks was markedly different in many respects.

Philip is certain that the animal he encountered was a Great White and, while he did not share this opinion with his boating colleagues on the day because he did not wish to alarm the youngsters, they have subsequently discussed the encounter and are all in agreement with his opinion.

Common and Grey Seals are abundant in that area and, to the west of North Uist, the Monach Islands have what is thought to be the largest seal colony in Europe. **N.B.** In September 2011 I spent 2 weeks on a shark search expedition based in Lochmaddy. The expedition attracted considerable local interest out of which came a report from a local fisherman of another sighting of what was thought to be a Great White Shark at the same time, and in the same place as Philip Harding's encounter. Sadly the witness, Angus John MacDonald had died in the meantime and so could not give me a firsthand account. However I interviewed his brother, Donald John MacDonald who was able to give me a very clear report of what his sibling had told him he saw. Angus was a sensible and highly experienced fisherman who would have known what he was looking at, and he was quite convinced that, like Philip Harding, he had seen a Great White Shark. The two sightings had happened within days of each other.

WESTERN ISLES SCOTLAND: JUNE 2007

Mathematician and marine scientist Jim Watson told me in June 2007 that he had been hearing regular reports of Great White Sharks in the Minch and Little Minch over the previous ten years. This fits with three of the more compelling accounts mentioned in this chapter. The Minch would be an ideal place for Great White Sharks: several Grey Seal colonies, and shoals of Haddock, Mackerel, Cod, Herring and Pollock provide an adequate food source, and the water temperatures (with summer highs of 16°C and winter lows of 5°-6°C) are comfortably within the tolerance range for these sharks for much of the year.

Jim has made more than 3000 dives and has worked extensively in the waters around the Hebrides off and on throughout his life. He accepts the possible presence of Great White Sharks in the Minch in an almost matter-of-fact manner. I formed the impression that he would be more surprised by the suggestion that they were not there than they were there.

Jim suggested I contact the Hebridean Whale and Dolphin Trust to see if it had any anecdotal or actual evidence of the presence of Great Whites. I spoke at length to

Dr Peter Stevick and became interested when he offered to send me a picture of a large shark caught in the Minch some years ago and hitherto unidentified. The photograph turned out to be of a Mako, so there was no new evidence to add to my files.

SOUND OF HARRIS, SCOTLAND: LATE JUNE/EARLY JULY 2007

Film footage taken in the Sound of Harris on a mobile phone, possibly showing a shark attacking a seal, was sent to the Marine Conservation Society for comment in September 2007. Thereafter, it was passed on to us at the Shark Trust.

I have examined the footage as have the following other experts: Ian Fergusson, Jeremy Stafford-Deitsch, Leonard Compagno, Henry Mollet and Chris Fallows. I have also interviewed one of the eyewitnesses to the event.

Fergusson and Compagno both felt that the percentage likelihood in favour of the shark being a Great White was 60 per cent while there was a 40 per cent possibility of it being a Shortfin Mako. The other three felt it could be either but favoured a Shortfin Mako. My own view is that it was either a Shortfin Mako or, more probably, a Porbeagle.

The witness, Darren Steadwood, was at sea with two friends when extensive splashing in the water 18 metres away attracted their attention. They went to investigate and discovered a seal thrashing about on the surface. They were in a deep channel and could see it apparently being tossed about but didn't catch sight of a shark other than occasional glimpses of what might have been a fin. The video seems to show blood but Darren doesn't remember seeing any at the time.

Darren's friend recorded the incident on his mobile phone. The activity stopped and nothing happened for about 30 seconds and then a fin broke the surface between seven and nine metres away. They went to investigate as the shark swam away from them. Then it turned and swam towards the boat, going underneath it and then disappearing. There was no sign of the seal, or any seal remains, which may indicate that it had survived the attack and escaped if, indeed, it was an attack. My own opinion of the seal footage is that it is possibly two seals fighting or playing.

Darren estimated the length of the shark at three metres or just over, and recalls a stout body with a dark grey black dorsal (top) side. No gills were noticed. Darren did not get a view of the shark's underside and does not remember seeing its eyes. His initial impression was not of the seal being attacked but of animals playing or maybe feeding, which is consistent with my opinion.

The footage shows a dorsal fin appearing from the left of the screen. The fin appears to have a slightly rounded apex with a straight down trailing edge and a curved forward edge. At this stage, the dorsal shape is certainly more representative of a Great White Shark than that of a Shortfin Mako. However, as the shark continues to move the footage becomes confusing because, at some angles, the apex of the dorsal appears more rounded. A caudal fin then comes into view and the shark at this point is swimming directly away from the photographer still moving across the screen from left to right.

There is still nothing conclusive and the next good 'side on' dorsal view shows a fin with a more rounded than pointed apex. The shark keeps swimming towards the right, disappears, then a caudal fin reappears followed by the dorsal. Thereafter, it turns around and starts swimming from the right to the left on an interception track with the boat.

The next good 'side on' of the dorsal once again seems to say "Great White Shark", with a more pointed apex and a straight-down, perhaps even slightly concave, trailing edge. The shark is swimming quite fast and possibly displaying excited behaviour. The seal has by now disappeared, so there is a possibility that the presence of seals out of sight below the water is influencing the shark's behaviour. The shark then swims right up to the vessel, possibly making contact with the hull, before swimming underneath, which is where the footage ends. The shark could have been a Great White Shark but, equally, it could have been a Shortfin Mako or, a Porbeagle.

It is interesting to note, that potential Great White Shark incidents that retain credibility after investigation are clustered in two areas: North Cornwall and the Western Isles (the Minch, Little Minch). There are only three possible Great White Shark incidents outside these areas that I am aware of – the Pentland Firth 'net capture and escape in 2004', the Falmouth angling incident of 1965, and the possible spy hopping off Looe in the 1970's.

ST IVES, CORNWALL: JULY 2007

On Thursday 26 July, Dr Oliver Crimmen was shown a clip of amateur video by the Sun newspaper. It was taken on a video camcorder by Nick Fletcher while holidaying in St Ives. The film showed a small pod of Common Dolphins making their way along the coast and, at the end of the sequence, a creature is clearly seen to breach. Dr Crimmen was quoted as saying: "It's definitely predatory and definitely big. I can't rule out a Great White."

I, too, was asked to confirm the identity. But it was impossible because the film was not clear enough. All that could be seen for sure was that it was a fish somewhere between 2.4 metres (8 feet) and 3.6 metres (12 feet) long doing a half-to-three-quarters breach displaying a white ventral side. Given the close presence of dolphins, they must come into the reckoning as must Basking, Porbeagle and Mako sharks.

If, as I do, you believe that Great Whites are occasional visitors to our shores then that possibility cannot be ruled out. However, saying they can't be ruled out is a long way from confirming that the image showed a Great White Shark, which is what the Sun inferred that I had done.

This sparked an extraordinary media frenzy and the Sun managed to string it out for a further eight days with all the other nationals and many regional papers joining in. Both the Monday and Tuesday editions of the paper carried front page pictures of Basking Shark's dorsal fins slicing through the waters off St Ives with various 'experts' identifying the fins as belonging to Great Whites. By Thursday, the Newquay Guardian's front page carried a picture of a Great White said to be taken off Towan Head, Newquay (See page 14). This was the first picture of a Great White to appear, but interest was waning and various other reports were hinting at doubts over where the photograph was taken. The photograph was later admitted to be a hoax.

During this time, the people of St Ives were, understandably, cashing in. Shark spotting boat trips were packed with excited tourists. Virtually everything that could float was taking to the sea to look for sharks. Cafes had maps of St Ives Bay on their walls with all the sightings marked. Shark ice creams, T-shirts and even shark-shaped pasties were produced to add to the fun and make the tills ring more frequently.

Nick Fletcher's original film clip had been forgotten by the time the story died. This was one of the most intense and long running shark sagas ever in the UK press, but was by no means based on compelling evidence.

The question remains: do Great White Sharks ever visit British waters? For me, the answer is "probably yes". However, there is still no hard evidence and, owing to the massive depletion rates the species has suffered (about 80 per cent), the chances of any such visit are slim and getting slimmer.

Chapter Three

SHARK ANGLING

Very few holidaymakers who visited Cornwall in 1961 are likely to have been aware that 6,286 sharks were caught by anglers off the county's coast that year. It was the highest annual number ever recorded by the Shark Angling Club based in Looe. Most of the catch were Blue Sharks, but in those days Mako, Porbeagle and Thresher Sharks were also caught regularly on rod and line.

Before 1953, comparatively few sharks were caught by recreational anglers in British waters. However, in 1952 the use of "rubby dubby" started to become widespread, and the Shark Angling Club of Great Britain was founded the following year. "Rubby dubby" is the British name used to describe what most of the rest of the world calls "chum" or, in Australia, "burley". Chumming, rubby dubbying and burleying all describe the laying of a scent trail in the water by using mashed-up oily fish such as mackerel and pilchard. They are placed in net bags and hung over the side of the boat. After a time, the oil floats to the surface, and the small pieces of fish that work their way through the mesh sink in the water. The heavier pieces sink faster and further while the lighter ones stay closer to the surface. The overall effect is that of a multi-layered scent highway. Many anglers add bran to the mixture. That also sinks in the water and it is believed to help the effectiveness of the chum trail.

The founding of the Shark Angling Club quickly established Looe as the shark capital of Britain, and, in the 1950s and 1960s, its shark angling fleet consisted of 25 full-time boats during the June to October season. Falmouth, Mevagissey, Polperro, Porthleven, Newlyn and Penzance also had shark angling fleets, and boats started working from Padstow, Boscastle and Bude on the north Cornish coast, as well as out of north and south Devon and some ports in Dorset.

In the mid-1960s, a dozen boats worked out of the Isle of Wight and Portsmouth targeting Threshers and Porbeagles. Today, Isle of Wight shark anglers rarely see a Porbeagle; Threshers have become their most commonly encountered species.The Pembrokeshire coast has long been a good place to catch Blue Sharks, and, in recent years, numbers caught there have, on a pro rata number of boats basis, been higher than anywhere else in the UK. Porbeagles are also caught there and the occasional Mako is encountered. Many north east coastal ports including Whitby, Hartlepool and Bridlington, have attracted shark anglers, with Soupfin Shark (Tope) being the main target, although Porbeagles have become more recent additions.

The world record for a Porbeagle Shark catch – 230 kgs (507 lbs) - was established by Chris Bennett in the Pentland Firth in March 1993 (See page 34). Shark angling was started in The Highlands in 1992 by the now defunct Big Game Club of Scotland with the Pentland Firth port of Scrabster serving as the base of activities. Chris is still shark angling and reports a good population of Porbeagles in the area, where live bait, Cod or Pollock is used instead of rubby dubby.

The shark most highly prized by anglers is probably the Mako. The British record Mako - weighing 227 kgs (500 lbs) - was caught off Looe in 1971 by Mrs J Yallop (Page 30).

It has already been mentioned that Porbeagles, Makos and Threshers are caught in much lower numbers than Blue Sharks. However, what these four species have in common in angling terms is that they are all caught by using rubby dubby, whereas Stary Smoothhounds, Nursehounds (aka Bull Huss) and Piked Dogfish (Spurdogs) are caught near the seabed without rubby dubby. Tope are also commonly caught off the bottom, too, but do respond to rubby dubby. Also known as the Soupfin Shark and the School Shark, the Tope is found off all Britain's coasts.

Since 1961, Looe Shark Angling Club figures for shark catches crashed but in 2011 numbers recovered and 616 sharks were caught and released. To put these figures into context one has to take into account not only numbers caught but fishing effort involved. The 1960's and 70's catches of up to 6286 sharks involved 18/20 full time

The Shark Angling Club can be found on the quay in east Looe. © Shark Angling Club

SHARK ANGLING CLUB

G.B. HEADQUARTERS of

LOOE'S MAIN

BOAT BOOKING AGENCY

SHARK · REEF · ½ DAY REEF

2+HR. MACKEREL

EVENING CONGER

BOOK HERE 01503 262642

S.A.C.G.B.

Mrs Yallop with her British record Mako in 1971. © Shark Angling Club

J Pottier with his 211kg (465lbs) Porbeagle caught in 1976. © Shark Angling Club

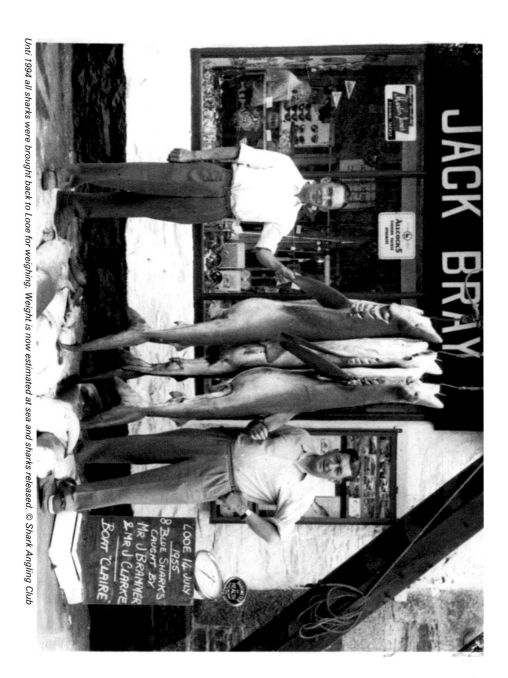

Until 1994 all sharks were brought back to Looe for weighing. Weight is now estimated at sea and sharks released. © Shark Angling Club

LOOE 14 JULY
1955
8 BLUE SHARKS
CAUGHT BY
MR J BRANNER
& MR J CLARKE
BOAT "CLAIRE"

A Blue Shark loses its battle. All SAC GB sharks are now released. © Shark Angling Club

Chris Bennett with his world record 507lbs Porbeagle Shark caught in the Pentland Firth March 1993. © Chris Bennett

angling boats. The 2011 figure of 616 involved 1 full time and 6 part time vessels. Therefore the figure of 616 is even more encouraging than it appears at first glance, and is a dramatic improvement on the low of 86 sharks caught in 2000. These improved figures are in contradiction to what we know is happening to Blue Sharks in the North Atlantic, and it may be that there are not more sharks but that shark movements have changed.The regular incidence of Mako, Porbeagle and Threshers has now become sporadic. There is no Shark Angling Club record of a Mako being caught since the 1970's and a juvenile Porbeagle caught in 2002 was the first caught by a club boat for many years. Threshers caught in 2005 and 2007 were also the first for several years. In fact, all of the species targeted by anglers in British waters have suffered severe population declines owing to commercial fishing pressures.

Trevor Housby's book "Shark Fishing in British Waters" (published in 1972) describes the Isle of Wight as the 'top Porbeagle hotspot yet discovered'. Danny Vokins is, perhaps, the most successful current Isle of Wight shark angler and he hasn't seen a Porbeagle in island waters since 1996. Blue and Soupfin (Tope) Sharks were so common in the 1960s that they were almost unchallenging nuisances to many anglers; today, they are highly prized. Housby's Isle of Wight top Porbeagle hotspot has become the best place in British seas to catch Threshers and in 2006 twelve were caught and tagged, while the figure for 2007 was twenty. I have talked about Porbeagles at greater length in Chapter 7 so suffice it to say here that most Porbeagle angling hotspots used to quickly become cold spots once the word got out and longliners moved in. In 2009 the European Union declared a zero Total Allowable Catch (TAC) for Porbeagles, and as long as this restriction remains in force Porbeagles have effective protection in Europe from targeted fisheries - bycatch is another matter altogether (see Chapter 13).

ANGLING EQUIPMENT

Much has been written about the equipment used by anglers to catch sharks. Brigadier J.A.L. Caunter, founder of the Shark Angling Club, stated that rods should be about seven foot long with plenty of play in the tip and strength in the butt. J.H. Bennet, in Big Game Angling, describes a rod as a spring between the fish, the power of the angler and the breaking strain of the line.

A visit to a London tackle shop acquainted me with a bewildering and diverse selection of big game rods. However, there are two basic types: the "stand up stick", a short, powerful rod used mainly for big game fish which dive deep, and the more common six-to-seven foot flexible rod that comes either in one or two pieces. The longer, more flexible rods are favoured by British shark anglers as they are better at coping with sharks making long runs near the surface and/or going under the boat from side to side. Early rods were made of hardwood, generally hickory. Thereafter, the progression went from copper, tubular steel, hollow glass and solid glass before manufacturers created today's carbon-fibre structures.

I am bound to upset someone if I say that American big game reels lead the world but it does seem that way. Wherever in the world I have talked to shark and big game anglers, I have come across the name Penn, short for the Penn Fishing Tackle and Manufacturing Company of Pennsylvania, or that of Shakespeare, which now appears to be the dominant force in reel manufacturing. Today's reels are complex, hi-tech pieces of kit fitted with brakes, drag governors, harness lugs and clutches. They are made of non-rust materials and often offer two speeds. Prices for heavy duty Penn reels range from £300 to £1500, so dropping a borrowed shark rod over the side should be avoided if one values one's friendship! Big game angling, including shark angling, is all about using the lightest line to catch the biggest fish. This ensures a battle of skill rather than a contest of strength. Basically, if the angler is not good enough and relies only on brute force the line will break and the fish will be lost. Sharks can easily bite through monofilament lines so, to prevent this, steel traces are used between the hook and the line. Yesterday's large, brutal barbed J-shaped hooks have been replaced by circle and barbless hooks, which are often biodegradable. These are designed to avoid deep or gut hooking sharks thus making removal easier.

CHANGING TIMES

In the 1960s in Looe it must have seemed as if the seas produced an endless supply of sharks. Most evenings during the season visitors to the quayside would have seen sharks hung up outside the Shark Angling Club (SAC) having been weighed and photographed with their captors. The following day most of the sharks were taken out to sea and dumped. In the 1960s and 1970s annual SAC catches of between 2,000 and 4,000 were usual. Throughout that period the club fleet comprised of 18–20 boats, all of which spent most of the season engaged in sharking.

Change was on the way though, and it arrived in 1976, when a catch of 928 was recorded compared with 2083 the previous year. This dramatic reduction of more than 50 per cent from one year to the next heralded a decline in numbers that bottomed out at the 86 caught in the year 2000. However, shark angling is not responsible for the decline as numbers caught by anglers around the world are insignificant compared with the tens of millions taken by industrial fishing. Having said that, even before the "crash of 76" attitudes in Looe were changing with more and more sharks being released each year. David Turner the author of 'The Shark Fisherman' remembers random tagging and releasing of young 30-60lb sharks during the 1960's. Then between 1972 and 1976, a tag-and-release programme was conducted as a joint effort by Dr John Stevens and the Shark Angling Club (the venture was part of Dr Stevens' Phd project) and 2,883 sharks – Blues, Soupfin Sharks (Tope), Porbeagles, and a Shortfin Mako - were tagged. Some years later the Jack Daniel's whiskey company took up sponsoring the next tag-and-release programme and all those returning tags with the requested information were rewarded with a bottle of whiskey. That sponsorship ended in 1995 and, from then on, all sharks caught were released unrecorded until tagging resumed under my sponsorship in August 1999.

To qualify to join the Shark Angling Club, an angler must land a catch weighing a minimum of 75lbs. This used to mean that all sharks that appeared to attain that weight or more had to be killed and weighed to enable new members to qualify. But, as I mentioned, attitudes were changing, and, in 1994, the club passed new rules involving a formula that enabled skippers to estimate weight based on length and girth. This rule came in specifically to stop the need for killing - unless a record was suspected, in which case the fish still had to be weighed. Other than suspected records, the club now operates a 100 per cent release policy and most skippers take part in the tagging programme.

One seeming contradiction among hunters of animals on land and sea is the respect and affection with which they regard their quarry. So the question is: why catch it? I suspect that question would get 10 different answers from 10 different individuals, but what would be uniform is the respect that I have observed first hand among 99 per cent of the shark anglers I know. One man who long lined large numbers of Porbeagles in December 2003 attracted widespread condemnation, with shark anglers being among the loudest critics. In August 2007, another longliner caught more than 80 sharks near Lundy Island and he, too, was universally derided by anglers. Those who take up shark angling as a blood sport are quickly identified as such by skippers and there is a virtual black list of people they will not take out again. Thankfully, it's a short list.

Changing attitudes have brought about differences to equipment, with the use of circle and barbless hooks now being the norm. Also, not all Looe skippers will tag sharks as some feel that removing the animals from the "support' of the water causes damage to organs that can prove fatal. This is correct and most skippers bring only the smaller sharks onboard, while tagging the larger ones over the side of the boat. All skippers are highly competent and hook removal, tagging, and measuring is done in the minimum of time. Survival rates among released Blue Sharks are thought by the Shark Angling Club to be near 100 per cent although it might possibly be less in the case of Porbeagles.

When a Shark Angling Club tagged shark is re-caught, the fisherman will find the tag has a "message in a bottle system", which offers a $15 reward for letting the club know the length of the shark and the latitude and longitude of its re-catch position. As it happens, 99 per cent of returns are from Spanish longliners operating in the Bay of Biscay and between the Azores and the Canaries. However, in 2002, the club was told about a female Blue Shark re-caught off the New Hampshire coast while other returns have come from the USA, South America and South Africa. Therefore, it can be clearly seen that tag and release helps establish migration patterns and provides information about growth rates.

Like others all over the world engaged in eco-tourism and leisure, the Shark Angling Club acknowledges the economic importance of sharks. The Great White Shark has become a recognised and valued asset in the South African Western Cape, and the Blue Shark has been part of Looe's economy for 50 years. So the more it's recognised that sharks have a greater value alive rather than dead, the more recruits will swell conservationist ranks.

To recap:
- Up to six thousand sharks caught each year off Looe dropped to 86, but catches are now increasing again

- Eighteen full-time boats have decreased to seven part-timers

- An almost total kill has become no kill

- The thriving drift net pilchard industry that attracted sharks and triggered them becoming targets for anglers has disappeared

- Hook sizes and designs have altered and angling club rules have changed

- Trophy photos have given way to tags

Commercial fishing policies are starting to change so hopefully shark numbers will begin to recover. If they do, no organisation will be happier than the Shark Angling Club.

I have concentrated largely on Shark angling off my home county of Cornwall where many of the skippers are known to me and research has been relatively easy. However mention must be made of increasing shark angling activity in other parts of Britain. In recent years Blue and Porbeagle Shark angling activity off the Penbrokeshire coast has been increasing, and in the summer of 2011 one angling boat caught and released 50 Blue Sharks in a single day.

The Scottish Sea Angling Conservation Network (SSACN) was started in 2006 and has expanded steadily since its founding. The main sharks targeted by SSACN anglers are Soupfin Sharks (Tope), Spurdogs, Starry Smoothhounds, and Nursehounds.

In 2011 the Shark Trust launched the Angler Recording Project which asked UK anglers to start recording all elasmobranchs (sharks, skates and rays) caught. The Trust commented "the aim of the project is not to stop anglers enjoying the excitement of catching sharks, skates and rays, but to gain a better understanding of their distribution and abundance – vital in making our fisheries sustainable".

Chapter Four

HUNTING THE GIANTS

Basking Shark Fisheries

Since the dawn of time man has hunted large animals. Mammoths, elephants, buffalo, and whales have all fallen prey to his traps, spears, arrows, snares and harpoons. However, early man did not kill for sport but to survive, finding uses for every part of his prey's body.

Reaching sizes of more than nine metres and weights of six to seven tonnes, the Basking Shark is truly a giant. The second largest fish in the world is a harmless plankton feeder, which at times has been hunted extensively. Man has found many uses for this gentle giant, including liver oil used as a lubricant and lamp oil, whilst squalene extracted from the oil has been used in cosmetics. Its skin has served as sandpaper and been used in making leather goods, while insulin has been extracted from the pancreas, flesh has been converted into fish meal and fins have ended up in soup. But perhaps the most bizarre use man has yet found for Basking Sharks was during in the Second World War, when Hurricane fighter pilots training in Scotland sometimes used them for target practise.

The first recorded Basking Shark fishery was on the island of Canna in the Sea of the Hebrides. Fisheries came and went probably due to fluctuations in abundance and market conditions for the products, and the peak of Basking Shark fishing in British seas was in the 1950s. Anthony Watkins was operating a fishery before the Second World War based at Carradale in the Kintyre Peninsula on the Firth of Clyde. He concentrated mainly on the oil extracted and was the first man to realise that static factories would not work. That was a mistake made by Gavin Maxwell – best known as author of the acclaimed wildlife book "Ring of Bright Water" - when he set up his factory on the island of Soay and it was probably one of the major factors in the failure of that enterprise. Watkins went to fight in the war and resumed his activities afterwards. He was the first man to operate a factoryship, which accompanied his fleet of three or four catcher boats, and a few remnants of his business about half-a-mile north of the little harbour at Port Crannaich exist to this day.

The rendering plant had to be sited far enough away from human habitation for the stench not to affect local people. Watkins concentrated on the livers and the remainder of the carcass was dumped and left to rot. His three boats ranged widely from the Firth of Clyde to the Hebrides during July, August and early September. In later years, in addition to the rendering plant, the Watkins factory ship was kitted out to be able to handle the livers as well, and, as a result, he could barrel his oil at sea and dispatch it to the mainland point of sale.

Basking Sharks were always harpooned and guns were mounted in the bows of the catching boats as was the case with whaling ships. Barbed harpoons were originally the most widely used and the Norwegian Kongsberg was considered the most successful gun. The harpoon was aimed either just behind or just ahead of the dorsal fin, the idea being to penetrate the body cavity. When the harpoon was pulled back the semi tubular barbs opened giving the harpoon a fix. As soon as the shark was harpooned it would dive for the bottom. Up to one hundred fathoms of stout five/seven centimetres thick manila rope would be fixed to the harpoon with the other end secured to the catching boat. Big sharks would often take their captors for a ride before dying. In later years, barrels were attached to the rope end, which effectively marked the harpooned sharks, leaving catching boats free to pursue further kills, returning later to collect their earlier victims.

It is possible that up to 100,000 Basking Sharks were killed in the Northeast Atlantic, including the British Isles, over the past century, but during both world wars there were let ups, which to a small degree allowed numbers to recover.

However, after World War Two a lot of things in Britain were in short supply, and Basking Shark oil fetched very good prices. One third of the volume of a Basking Shark is its bilobal (two lobes) liver, which contains the oil. The liver acts as a hepatic float that helps control flotation and buoyancy. Oil extraction was achieved either by rendering (boiling down) or by using centrifuges.

Dorsal fin. UK Basking Sharks now enjoy protection, but the fin trade is driving sharks to the brink of extinction in many places. © Colin Speedie 2005

Typical tadpole shaped head of a young shark feeding. © Colin Speedie 2005

A feeding shark. © Colin Speedie 2005

Basking Sharks are often seen breaching, which is generally assumed to be associated with courtship and/or with attempts to get rid of parasites. © Colin Speedie 2006

45

Remains of Maxwell's factory on Soay. © Colin Speedie 2004

In addition to the fisheries in the Hebrides and off the West coast of Ireland, some attempts were made to catch these giants off Cornwall. Colin Speedie, the Basking Shark researcher and conservationist, tells of an incident involving a boat in the 1930s. A small powerboat went out from Portscatho and harpooned a shark that then towed the crew 16 miles out to sea before they had to cut it free to avoid ending up in Ireland or the United States! In the 1960s a Cornish pig farmer killed about 16 sharks and landed them on the flats at Mylor with a view to cutting them up and using them for pig feed. But one got some revenge, having been kicked by the farmer who was checking to see if it was dead. It wasn't and it flicked its tail giving its captor a hefty thump.

The Norwegians were notable Basking Shark hunters and had dedicated shark fishing fleets, as they did for whaling. Average catch records showed a three-to-one ratio of females to males, a figure that was much higher in the records of Gavin Maxwell. From the 1950s, some Basking Sharks caught in British waters were used to supply the Far East fin trade and this continued into the 1970's, although they were also then coming from Ireland. It is fortunate that the methods of killing were not more efficient during the period in question, or the already mentioned figure of around 100,000 sharks killed in the 20th century would certainly be much higher. Interestingly, the hunters knew their prey by different names. To Scottish fishermen the shark is known as Muldoan, meaning "sunfish" or "sailfish", the Gaelic name is Cearban and the Nordic name is Brugde. Ken Watterson, an Isle of Man based Basking Shark researcher working in the 1980/90's, called his first research boat Gobbag Vooar, which is Manx Gaelic for big mouth.

One of the best documented accounts of Basking Shark fishing is that of Gavin Maxwell's enterprise on Soay. Although best known for "Ring of Bright Water", Maxwell wrote several other books and his "Harpoon at a Venture" is the history of his time as a Hebridean shark fisherman. The book provides lots of valuable information about post-war British Basking Shark hunting and the sale of products derived from them. In 1945 Basking Shark oil was selling for £80 a tonne, and it was a rising market. By 1947, prices had increased to £110. An average shark would produce 358 kilos, which made each animal worth about £45 in oil. All these amounts were a great deal of money 65 years ago.

On one occasion Maxwell records trying to kill a shark using a Breda light machine gun, which he kept on board to deal with mines left over after the war. Maxwell's first kill was a female measuring eight metres overall, with a girth of more than five metres and a tail just under two metres across. The head was one-and-a-half metres from the nose tip to the first gill slit, and the dorsal fin just under one metre. A big fish by any standards but not as big as they get. Colin Speedie has seen two or three sharks he estimated to be nearly 12 metres long.

Maxwell acknowledged that he made two big mistakes in his venture. Firstly, he had to transport all the sharks back to his factory at Soay. That was expensive and hugely time consuming – a factory ship with the catching boats would have been the answer. Secondly, he dealt in too many products - liver oil, frozen flesh, salted flesh, liver residue, dried fins, bone manure etc - instead of just concentrating on the most valuable. The sharks he caught were towed back to Soay and positioned at the factory slipway; a small railway led from the sea to the cutting up area. The carcasses were floated on to a bogie truck moving on rails and hauled up the incline by a large steam winch. Once on the cutting floor, sharks would be skinned by workers wearing armoured gloves to protect them from the abrasive skin, and then their livers would be removed. They would then be cut up and pieces placed in barrels at the oil extraction plant. The fins were put in tanks for the extraction of glue liquor, whilst the flesh went into the ice house. Remains of the Soay factory still exist (See page 46).

Watkins and Maxwell were competitors and often hunted in the same areas. In the four years that Maxwell caught Basking Sharks he killed seven females for every male, and recalls on several occasions seeing males with claspers (external sexual organs) about a metre long and 18cm thick. However as the researcher Ken Watterson observed lampreys normally attach themselves in the genital area and it is possible that on occasions lampreys were mistaken for claspers.

In 1946 a Chinese businessman wrote to Maxwell offering money for sharks' fins, pointing out the high value these could achieve due to their perceived aphrodisiac values. It's believed this could be one of the first instances of the fin trade coming to Britain. During Maxwell's time on Soay, the Sweeneys of County Mayo, on the West coast of Ireland, sent a representative to consult with him as they, too, were planning to establish a Basking Shark fishery. At the end of 1946 under capitalisation caused Maxwell to sell out for £13,550. He became managing director of the new company and got a shareholding as part of the deal.

The need for having a factory ship was sharply brought home on one occasion in particular when, in two days, Maxwell's boats killed 15 sharks 70 miles from Soay. The time needed for ferrying them to the on-shore factory would have been prohibitive so he decided to beach them on the island of Scalpay. There, his men cut out the livers, putting them in herring barrels to transport them back to base. This method of working continued and a small steamer was hired to transport the barrels.

By the end of the 1947 season the company decided to use spotter planes and a factory ship was to begin operations the following year. However, neither plan actually materialised and Maxwell resigned in July 1948. In 1949, his successor put the company's assets up for sale. Maxwell's gunner Tex Geddes, bought some of the gear and continued as a freelance shark fisherman, enjoying moderate success.

The shark whose oil once lit the streets of Dublin and provided targets for the RAF to practise on is now under most threat in our waters from accidental "by-catch" in fixed fishing gear such as gill nets and lobster pot ropes, together with collisions with leisure craft users. Jet skiers, water skiers and boaters sometimes come into contact with Basking Sharks feeding at the surface, especially around headlands, and every year injuries are recorded. On occasions, the sharks are rammed deliberately but, in the main, the contact is accidental.

In August 1999 when I was on a day trip to Lundy Island off North Devon, our ferry narrowly missed a Basking Shark as we approached the jetty. Fins were visible all across the bay and we observed fins from the cliff tops in several places as we walked around the island. Cliff walkers in parts of Devon, Cornwall, the Isle of Man, and the Western Isles often have the opportunity of seeing these creatures. The Shark Trust offers a code of conduct series of guidelines to boat operators for observing the sharks while avoiding disturbing or endangering them.

Until recently, it was believed that their disappearance in the winter months indicated that Basking Sharks hibernated. In 2003 studies (Sims et al) disproved this theory and showed that, in fact, the sharks spent more time at depth of up to 900 metres feeding on deepwater plankton. Satellite tagging (Sims et al again) has shown that Basking Sharks move thousands of miles during the winter months tracking plankton blooms to feed. In 2007 a Basking Shark tagged near the Isle of Man revealed that these sharks make transatlantic crossings (Dr. Mauvis Gore and colleagues).

Basking Sharks are now completely protected in British seas out to the 12-mile limit and the only humans hunting them are doing so for purposes of eco-tourism (See chapter 5). In 2002, the species received Appendix II listing from the Convention on International Trade in Endangered Species (CITES) and was listed on Appendix I of the Bonn Convention on Migratory Species (CMS) in 2005. In addition, there is a UK Biodiversity Action Plan for Basking Sharks.

The Killer Whale and the Great White Shark are both known to attack Basking Sharks but pose nothing like the threat that industrial fishing did. Colin Speedie hopes that numbers may slowly be starting to recover from the lows reached during the last century, when man hunted this gentle giant.

A new twist to shark eco-tourism. Cartoon Chris Wylie.

Chapter Five

SHARK ECO-TOURISM

In the 1970's Porbeagle sharks off Crackington Haven in North Cornwall were in such abundance that angling boats used to queue to drift chum the reef. Whenever I recall that situation, I think what a shame it was that those anglers were killing their catches, and not just observing them. With the numbers that used to exist then, cage diving would have been possible as long as the sharks cooperated and, if the sharks had been examined and admired rather than overfished, they would still be plentiful.

Annual catches of Blue Sharks by the Looe angling fleet were once 2000, 3000, 4000, 5000...even, in one year, 6000 and, although the number has now dropped, there are still angling boats that pursue both Blues and Porbeagles on Cornwall's north and south coasts. In South Africa's Western Cape yesterday's fishermen and trophy anglers have become today's shark guardians and eco-tourism operators. So why can't the same mentality rule in Britain? Although vastly depleted, we've still got the sharks, and we've got the angling boats, so why couldn't we do the same? If cage diving were to prove possible it would be a win for the sharks, a win for the skippers, a win for holidaymakers and shark enthusiasts - and a win for eco-tourism!

In August 2005, my wife, Jacqui, and I decided to see if shark eco-tourism would work in the UK. Together with groups of volunteers, we ran two pilot days out of Looe, aware of the sceptical glances of skippers peering suspiciously and doubtingly at our chum slick. No baited hooks and multiple floats, just the usual chum bags over the side and another one with a float on a line 15 metres astern. The first shark arrived after 40 minutes and the second an hour-and-a-half later. A large two-and-a-half metre Blue Shark grabbed our bait bag and we had a tug of war. I lost, the bag ripped and our shark had breakfast, lunch and supper all in one go.

We steamed back to Looe and on the way I spotted and rescued a net-entangled porpoise. Two Blue Sharks, a number of dolphins, and a porpoise rescue - not a bad day. The following weekend we drew a blank but one out of two is 50 per cent, and we decided to take the idea further and run a proper pilot project in the summer of 2006 with three Blue Shark days out of Looe, and three Porbeagle days out of Bude and Padstow. We sent two press releases to the diving magazines which resulted in short, one paragraph items - and we also put the idea on our website. The response was phenomenal: the phone rang constantly and our email box filled up. Thereafter, we had to double our planned six days to 12 with six participants per day. All in all, around 2,000 people enquired after 72 places. There was no doubt that the interest was there!

The winter was spent planning and plotting. Two shark cages were built, and I designed a special "hook over the gunnels" dive platform and steps. Many enquirers questioned the necessity for cages for Blues and Porbeagles. However, both are predatory animals and while, as far as I know, there are no confirmed records of Porbeagle attacks, there are records of Blues being dangerous to humans so safety was a vital factor. Other considerations were how to provide stability in the water in Cornwall's surface currents, and how to keep the sharks around the boats. In the past, I have deployed a rope line to hang onto, which, with a float on it tucked under an arm, provided hands-free anchorage but not total stability. Caging our participants not only provided total safety for both sharks and humans, but also solved the stability problem and enabled me to bait the animals safely right up to the cage. The limiting factor for using cages is the lumpy north Atlantic where the sea state often makes the use of cages too dangerous. When conditions are too bad for caging I get into the water with my shark billy, and 2/3 people at a time swim with the sharks.

I knew I could attract Blues to a cage (see page 53), or to swimmers, but Porbeagles are shy and my previous attempts to get into the water with them had failed. One of those attempts gained me a brief glimpse and the other was a washout, resulting in no sighting at all. A human finning around struggling to

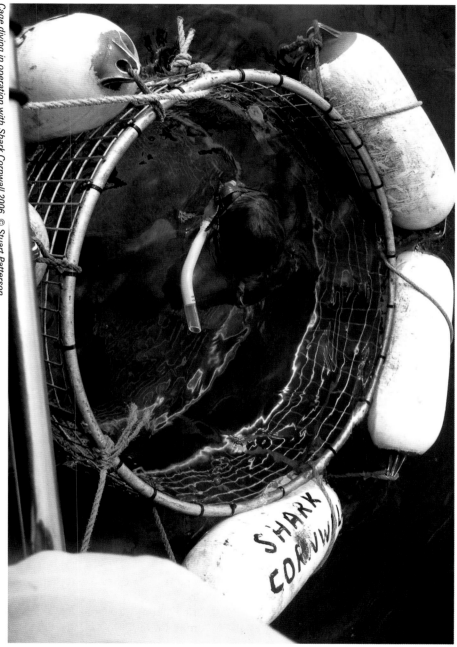

SHARK CORNW

Our secret weapon, the mirrored chum tube. © Tony Bennett

A man's eye view of a Blue Shark cruising past the cage. Shark Cornwall 2006. © M. Boothman

Swimming with Basking Sharks. © Atlantic Divers

maintain position in a five-knot current is not going to result in calm sharks, and, generally, they are unlikely to hang around long after a snorkeller gets in the water. As soon as we started chumming, I planned to put the cage into the water so there would be no splash or disturbance when the sharks arrived. I hoped then to slip our observers into the cage, and keep the shark around it. Provided conditions were flat enough, it seemed cages would be the best way forward for all these reasons.

The 2006 pilot project went well and a great deal was learned. The success rate in encountering Blue Sharks was 66 per cent on the north coast. In 2007, we expanded the project to more than 50 days, which meant we could take out more than 300 participants. As it happened, a summer of unsettled weather meant that we lost half our planned days but the encounter success rate remained at a similar level. In short, we had proved the concept worked and that a profitable eco-tourism opportunity was there to be developed. We have continued taking enthusiasts to sea to cage dive and snorkel with Blue Sharks, and in 2009 our friends, Chris and Annabelle Lowe of Atlantic Divers borrowed one of our cages and started taking trips out from Newquay. I am aware of operators in south Cornwall and Pembrokeshire also starting cage diving so hopefully it is taking off.

The limiting factors are the short season of only 3 months from July to September, our lumpy seas and unsettled weather. I have kept records of our days between 2006-2011 inclusive, and in the 6 year period we cancelled just over 50% of our August trips. For cage diving or swimming with the sharks better conditions are needed than for angling, and this loss of earning days is one of the main reasons that more shark angling skippers haven't become cage diving operators. Conditions in South Africa's western Cape are broadly similar but shark eco-tourism is viable there as they have a season which lasts the whole year as opposed to our 3 months.

Shark angling can also be classed as eco-tourism and opportunities to take part are many and diverse. In the southwest of England Looe, Padstow, Falmouth, Mevagissey, Bude, St Ives, Newquay, Penzance, Plymouth, Clovelly, Hartland and many other fishing harbours offer shark angling. In Pembrokeshire, Porbeagle and Blue Shark fishing is possible in at least three places. The Isle of Wight provides opportunities to encounter Thresher Sharks as do the Channel ports. Soupfin Shark (Tope) fishing is common all around the British Isles with many good spots in particular on the North Sea coast. The rugged and dramatic Pentland Firth is where the world record Porbeagle Shark was caught and the little port of Scrabster, next to Thurso, has two boats that can be chartered for shark angling.

After angling, the largest and best established shark eco-tourism in British seas is Basking Shark watching. There are three hotspots for this activity and all offer good chances of sightings. However, the big difference between watching Basking Sharks and baiting sharks for cage diving is that with Basking Shark watching operators cannot create opportunities. The sharks are either on the surface and visible or they are not, and, if they are not, there is nothing anyone can do about it, whereas with baiting or chumming the operator has an element, a small element, of control or influence.

Cornwall, the Isle of Man and North West Scotland (the Sea of the Hebrides) are the three best locations in Britain for spotting Basking Sharks. Sometimes they can be seen from the shore but the best chance of success lies in going to sea armed with a pair of binoculars. Operators offering Basking Shark watching trips can easily be found in the three areas mentioned. Some offer viewing only from boats whereas others specialise in putting experienced people in the water to snorkel with these huge sharks. Typically, snorkellers will be dropped in the water near the sharks and the operators' boat will then move away to minimise disturbance, and negate the possibility of upsetting the sharks.

The common perception is that Basking Sharks are harmless, however any animal that grows up to 10 metres, and can weigh the same as a single-decker bus should be treated with caution and respect. In June 2009 I was snorkelling with Baskers and felt threatened enough to decide to get out of the water. I don't know how many hours I have spent in the water with Basking Sharks in the past 18 years, but I can say with some confidence that it's more than a hundred. We were about four miles off Newquay and saw at least 30 sharks on the surface, feeding in small groups. The sharks were breaching regularly, and females made up the majority of the group. There were six of us swimming and free-diving, and everyone was well behaved – there was no chasing of, or swimming at, the sharks. The smallest shark I saw was about 4m long, so there were no pups as far as I was aware.

At the end of our first swim, three sharks appeared below me at the edge of my visibility at a depth of 6-8 m. They circled me, then slowly tightened their circle and rose in the water, getting closer all the time. There was clearly a purpose to this manoeuvre. Their swimming became faster and more purposeful and I began to feel threatened by the sharks. Chris and Annabelle Lowe of Atlantic Divers watched the incident from the boat, and felt the behaviour of the sharks was purposeful and potentially dangerous. Quite correctly Chris called everyone out of the water but most went back in soon afterwards, and there was no repetition of the sharks' earlier behaviour. They swam by with mouths open, filter-feeding as they went. Why did the sharks behave like this? I simply don't know; maybe there were pups around that I didn't see; maybe weird, ungainly human forms were seen as competitors for the food source; maybe they were just telling me to buzz off; or maybe we had made mistakes we weren't aware of. The lesson is: enjoy them, but be careful. We are the guests in their environment.

With the huge increase in public interest in marine wildlife in general and sharks in particular, shark eco-tourism in Britain is certain to expand. Eco-tourism has two enormous values to the cause of shark conservation. Firstly, it provides a great opportunity to increase public awareness of sharks in a balanced and positive way thereby promoting conservation values; and, secondly, live sharks can provide earning opportunities day after day whereas one that is dead only has a one-time value. The fact is that man will protect wildlife if there's money in it for him.

The following is the Cage Diving Code of Conduct that I wrote for the Shark Trust. It may give readers an insight into how this form of eco-tourism works, and provide a guide as to what to look for when selecting an operator.

CODE OF CONDUCT FOR CAGE DIVING OPERATORS

The term "cage diving" is a misnomer because diving itself is not involved. Participants enter a cage that, typically, will be no more than three metres in depth,and then go to the bottom of it for viewing. Snorkelling, breathholding, and air lines from scuba tanks are used and in all cases, the participant's head is less than a metre below the surface.

This code of conduct is not intended as a comprehensive set of safety rules but is to promote good practice in interaction with sharks. At the time of writing shark diving takes place all over the world, but the most popular destinations include South Africa, Isla Guadeloupe, South Australia, California (Great White Sharks),Cornwall (Basking and Blue Sharks), Bermuda, the Caribbean and South Africa (Tiger Sharks, reef sharks, etc.).

GOOD PRACTICE.
1. Legal (dependent on local laws) products only should be used in shark chumming
2. Cages should be robust enough to withstand mouthing or accidental bumping by the sharks (Great White Sharks)
3. Viewing ports should be large enough for good viewing and photography, but not large enough to permit entry of sharks into the cage
4. Sharks should not be fed as there is evidence that this can lead to "conditioned" behaviour
5. Sharks should not be allowed to bite baits, bait tubes or chum sacks

6. Sharks should not be teased or worked into a frenzy so that they behave like circus animals
7. Sharks should not be touched or handled by operators - eg, Great White Sharks are often baited to the side of boats, and then teased into putting their heads out of the water so that operators can grab their noses prior to pushing them back into the water
8. Sharks should not be touched or handled by those in cages
9. When drawing baits towards cages to bring sharks close to participants, care should be taken not to make them charge after the bait thereby producing the risk of crashing into or colliding with the cage possibly resulting in injury to the sharks and/or the participants
10. Baits should be kept away from propellers and other sharp objects to avoid injuries to sharks
11. Participants should be advised at the start of the trip that calm surface conditions are necessary for safe cage entry/exit, and that, in the event of it not being possible to deploy the cage, participants will be restricted to watching the sharks from the deck and/or snorkelling in small groups with appropriate safety measures being taken.
12. Closed-top cages must be capable of easy, quick opening from inside
13. Participants should never be allowed to wear their own wetsuits. If they insist then operators should ensure they are thoroughly washed after the dive. (Clearly it would not be a good idea for people on holiday to be cage diving one day in their own wetsuit and get it thoroughly impregnated with the smell of chum, and then to go surfing the next day in areas where there are sharks that might endanger them)
14. Operators must allow for the direction of their chum slicks in terms of influence on non-related activities. For example, drawing inshore sharks out to sea away from bathers is obviously safe. However, a chum slick going across a bathing beach could bring sharks into contact with bathers
15. Being in contact with the public gives operators the opportunity to promote shark conservation to their clients. It is urged that education and conservation be made part of the cage diving experience.

Below is a list of operators working at the time of writing. It is not complete and I apologise to anyone I have left out.

Location/Activity/Operator/Contact.
Looe, Cornwall. Shark Angling - Shark Angling Club
Padstow, Cornwall. Shark Angling - Padstow Angling Centre
Bude, Cornwall. Cage diving – Shark Cornwall
Penzance, Cornwall. Basking Shark Watching - Marine Discovery

Penzance, Cornwall. Basking Shark Watching - Elemental Tours
Newquay, Cornwall. Basking Shark Watching – Atlantic Divers
Newquay, Cornwall. Cage diving – Atlantic Divers
Bude, Cornwall. Cage diving – Bude Boat Charter
St. Keverne, Cornwall. Basking Shark Watching - Porthkerris Divers
St Keverne, Cornwall. Basking Shark Watching - Dive Action
Bude, Cornwall. Shark Angling - Bude Boat Charter
Peel, Isle of Man. Basking Shark Watching - Various
Pembroke Docks, Milford Haven. Shark Angling - Various
Scrabster, near Thurso, Scotland. Porbeagle Angling - Various

I have not included websites and other contact points because this is not intended to be a directory. It is merely to provide guidance as to where to start looking.

The South African model shows how economically important shark eco-tourism can be. In January 2008 my friend Craig Ferreira in South Africa told me that the twelve cage diving operators were generating over 70 million rand (£5,400,000) per year i.e. approximately £450,000 per operator, and these figures increased dramatically in 2010 when South Africa hosted the football World Cup. This is the direct revenue being taken by the operators, the value of the industry is much larger once all the tangential aspects have been considered. Hotel rooms, shuttle buses, restaurants, airlines, retailers, and a host of others benefit directly from tourists coming to South Africa to see sharks. We can do some similar figures for Cornwall. In 2007 we had over 300 clients booked for cage diving at £95 per head. This is £28,500 of direct revenue and can be doubled if one assumes that each person spent another £100 in the county. We did only four days a week with six people a day, so on this basis it's easy to see how one operator working seven days a week, and taking out eight to ten clients daily would comfortably produce over £100,000 a year for himself and other benefiting businesses. I believe Cornwall could easily support ten operators which would mean a million pounds in revenue from cage diving. This figure would increase were Basking Shark watching revenue added, and I believe the only thing preventing shark eco-tourism becoming a huge earner for Cornwall is unsettled weather. The Shark Angling Club based in Looe, Cornwall now operates 7 shark angling boats and another 3 work independently, and for the last fifty-three years shark angling has been a major contributor to Looe's economy.

You can only kill something once, so dead value is one time, whereas live value is a day after day income stream. I am a cynic and believe that mankind is such an awful out of control species that unless it's in his interest not to do so he will end up killing most wildlife. Money is a great incentive not to kill. It's simple "if it pays it stays". That's why we have to develop shark eco-tourism and give sharks a real live value.

Chapter Six

BLUES, TOPE, ANGELS, HOUNDS, DOGS AND CATS

Blue Sharks, Soupfin Sharks (Tope), Angelsharks, Smoothhounds, Starry Smoothhounds, Spiny Dogfish (Spurdog), Nursehounds, Small Spotted Catsharks.

THE BLUE SHARK (Prionace glauca)

The first time I saw a Blue Shark was in the 1960s, while angling off Looe in South Cornwall. In those days, shark anglers killed what they caught, and they could not have foreseen the tragic collapse in shark populations that has occurred since. As I have said, angling has barely contributed to this position. Nevertheless, I am sure that those who killed what they caught now look back with regret.

The Blue Shark is probably the most wide ranging shark seen in British waters. Animals tagged off Cornwall and southern Ireland have often later been identified on the eastern seaboard of the United States, and those tagged in the North Atlantic have been recaptured in the South Atlantic. Blue Sharks are truly oceanic nomads and tagging programmes have helped establish the amazing journeys they undertake. It appears that mating occurs mostly on the western side of the

Atlantic and the males largely remain there while the females set off on an ocean crossing. Whether all impregnated females make this journey has not been established, but all the evidence points to them getting impregnated in the western Atlantic and then pupping on the eastern side. My own observations off Cornwall certainly bear this out as all the larger sharks I come across are females together with a lot of juveniles. I have on more than one occasion heard of rod-and-line caught pregnant females pupping on deck and all the baby sharks, together with mother, being quickly returned to the water and swimming off satisfactorily.

After copulation, males and females go their separate ways. The females store the sperm in their shell glands, and then self-fertilise several months later. However, the circular, round-trip migration route is not undertaken by all Blue Sharks all the time, and the picture is complicated by a degree of north-south migration. This involves sharks of both sexes and all ages and sizes.

As more tagging is carried out and more data becomes available, it is evident that Blue Shark movement patterns in the Atlantic are highly complex. North Atlantic Blue Sharks don't necessarily remain north of the equator: a shark tagged off Salcombe in Devon was recaptured three years later in the South Atlantic not far from the bulge of Brazil. Scientists don't have conclusive evidence as to how Blue Sharks navigate. However, experiments have shown that they can sense the earth's magnetic field and indications are that somehow, this ability may be used to chart their courses. Blue Sharks are mainly nocturnal feeders and tend to hunt in deeper waters. Herring, hake, bluefish and mackerel are all regular prey for western Atlantic dwelling sharks, and squid, octopus, cod, smaller sharks, pollock, and haddock are on the menu on the British side of the ocean. They will scavenge, and floating whale carcasses in particular get their attention.

The vision that comes to most minds on hearing the word shark is that of a Great White, which is many people's favourite and their idea of the perfect shark. For me, though, two British species are real "sharky" sharks. The enigmatic, stout, powerful "Great White like" Porbeagle is a challenging and captivating creature, and the electric blue, slim, sleek almost serpentine Blue Shark is an equal favourite (see page 66).

The Blue Shark is also called the Great Blue and on the rare occasions I have seen specimens larger than three metres, it was easy to see why. I have swum with these sharks off Cornwall, in the Mediterranean, and off South Africa and California. They may not be as menacing as Great Whites, Tiger or Bull Sharks but they must be respected as potentially dangerous. I once had one grab my fin and while it let go quickly and I thought it was funny at the time, I later realised the shark didn't know that my fin wasn't my ankle, which would not have been funny.

A Blue Shark, one of my favourites. © Richard Peirce

Smallspotted Catshark. © Sally Sharrock

Angel Shark. © Simon Rogerson

In baited situations, the shark is responding to the "ringing of the dinner bell" and it can certainly present threats. This was clearly illustrated on the last day of 2007, when I spent a magical few hours chumming for sharks off Cape Point with my friends Chris and Monique Fallows. By the end of a four-hour period, we had attracted more than 20 Blue Sharks, over 10 Makos, and a large (more than three metres) brown shark, which was either a Dusky Shark or a Bronze Whaler. There was enough bait and chum in the water to promote very excited behaviour and small Blue Sharks were behaving aggressively, competing for food with much larger Makos and showing no fear at all. The degree of excited, aggressive and competitive behaviour caused us to cease our activities before any sharks got hurt or damaged by colliding with the dive platform or a propeller. The experience graphically illustrated two points. Shipwreck victims injured, bleeding and struggling in the water could be in serious trouble in the presence of Blue Sharks, and eco-tourist operators working in chummed situations should know what they are doing, and err on the side of caution when making decisions.

The Blue Shark must keep moving. It has large pectoral fins that act like wings, the liver acts as a buoyancy device, and a powerful tail with a large upper lobe works as the propulsion unit keeping the shark in motion. Tests compared the efficiency of a 2.1 metre Blue Shark to that of a submarine, and, on a weight comparison basis, the shark required six times less propulsive power. These sharks are fast and have been recorded achieving speeds of up to 39.5 kph and travelling 71 kilometres in a day.

Due to the massive migrations Blue Sharks undertake and their dispersal throughout most of the world's oceans, they are probably the most fished shark species. Also, instead of several separate populations being exploited by different fisheries, we now suspect that the north Atlantic is just one population involved in a complex series of migration patterns and being depleted by fisheries on every route.

THE SOUPFIN SHARK (TOPE) (Galeorhinus galeus)

I don't know why but the word Tope sounds a little dull and doesn't really conjure up an image of a shark. Soupfin Shark not only sounds better but also the use of this name is a continual reminder of why sharks are being killed all around the world in unsustainable numbers, hence my use of this less common name.

The fish is also known as the School Shark, Vitamin Shark and the Oil Shark, and the name Tope probably derives from its taupe colour. The Soupfin Shark is caught on rod and line around most of the British coast. Fishing history was made in May 2002, when an albino Soupfin Shark was caught more than 129 kilometres from the Cornish coast. Albino sharks are extremely rare and so there was great excitement when this ghostly looking creature turned up in a trawl.

As with the Blue Shark, tagging programmes have established that the Soupfin Shark is a long distance traveller. The UK Shark Tagging Programme and others have produced solid evidence of the extent of their movements. Soupfin Sharks tagged in the English Channel, Irish Sea, and off Scotland's west coast have been recaptured off Spain, Portugal and Morocco, the Azores and the Canary Islands. One Soupfin Shark was known to have travelled more than 1770 kilometres in 62 days. Tagging results also seem to indicate that female sharks head south for warmer water pupping sites while males remain in northerly waters. Soupfin Sharks mainly live close to the seabed and have been recorded in depths of up to 400 metres. They are opportunistic feeders whose diet consists of bony fish and invertebrates, and they often find themselves part of the diet of larger sharks.

Soupfin Sharks are thought to have pups every two or three years with litter sizes of up to 50. As one of their names makes clear, they are often found in schools, which makes them vulnerable to fishing and angling. Tagging has also helped to establish that Soupfin Sharks are long living and probably attain ages of up to 60 years old.

This beautiful, slender, grey brown shark is fished all over the world for its liver oil, meat and fins, which has resulted in many populations being seriously depleted.

ANGELSHARK (Squatina squatina)

The Angelshark is not most people's idea of a shark. It is a large, stocky, flat fish that wouldn't win any beauty contests judged by those thinking of shapes more commonly associated with sharks. It can reach lengths of approaching two-and-a-half metres and has a grey to reddish brown dotted and spotted topside. This "ambush predator" spends most of its day lying buried on the seabed with its eyes protruding. It moves off the bottom at night and is a strong swimmer. The upper skin surface of the Angelshark is covered with spiky-shaped dermal denticles (tiny, tooth-like structures), whereas the underside has flattened scale-like denticles, which protect it as it swims over obstacles on the seabed. It is also one of those sharks capable of pumping water over its gills without swimming.

This species is severely depleted in much of its range; however in March 2008 it finally received protection out to six nautical miles under the Wildlife and Countryside Act. This was extended to 12 nautical miles at the end of 2011. This applies only to English and Welsh waters and similar protection is hoped for in Scotland and Northern Ireland. In December 2006 the Angelshark was declared locally extinct in the North Sea by ICES (the International Council for the Exploration of the Seas). Also sometimes known as Monkfish, this shark produces up to 25 pups following an eight to 10 month gestation period, and pupping in British seas usually occurs in mid summer. There is a record of its usual diet of flat fish, skates, crustaceans, and molluscs, having at least once been augmented by a cormorant!

STARRY SMOOTHHOUND
(Mustelus asterias)

The first edition of this book listed Smoothhounds and Starry Smoothhounds as two separate species both of which were present in UK waters. Subsequent research by Dr. Ed Farrell of the Fisheries Science Services Marine Institute, Galway Ireland, raised the question of whether both species do occur or whether we only have the Starry Smoothhound as a British species. As part of Farrell's research over 800 Smoothhounds from all over the Northeast Atlantic were sampled, of which 10% had no white spots (stars) and so were thought to be Common Smoothhounds. However these sharks were all reliably confirmed as being Starry Smoothhounds which raised the question of whether Common Smoothhounds occur in our waters.

Dr Farrell contends that it is very difficult to actually prove Common Smoothhounds do not occur, but suggests that until firm evidence is presented they should be considered as absent or vagrant.

It appears likely that the reason for assuming the presence of Common Smoothhounds was misidentification due to the absence of spots (stars) on some specimens which caused them to be identified as Common Smoothhounds.

The Starry Smoothhound is a favourite for keeping in captivity, where, with good husbandry, it does well and has been known to breed. These sharks reach sizes of up to 1½ metres and whilst they are not commercially targeted to any degree at the moment, there is concern that this may change. Starry Smoothhounds are found all around our coasts.

SPINY DOGFISH (Squalus acanthias)

The Spiny Dogfish is also known as the Spurdog, Piked Dogfish, the Doggy, and, to many fish and chip shop customers, as Rock Salmon. This slender shark can reach sizes of up to two metres and is listed by the International Union for the Conservation of Nature (IUCN) as "endangered" in British seas. I always think the nickname "dogfish" is a slightly unfair way of describing this nearly two metre bluish grey shark; "dogfish" certainly doesn't have the same ring to it as "shark" does!

The Spurdog is found almost all over the world and was once probably the most abundant species. Like the Starry Smoothhound, it is an aquarium favourite, and it is also targeted by sports anglers. Some Spurdogs undertake north-south migrations and others are resident all year round. It is thought that the species is depleted in British waters by over 90%, but from 2009 a series of measures were introduced which it is hoped will lead to recovery (See chapter 14).

The Spurdog is extremely long living and may reach 100. However, its late maturity, between 10 and 25 years-old, added to its habit of schooling, makes it particularly vulnerable to fisheries. I earnestly hope that the Spurdog doesn't join the Angelshark in being declared extinct in some British seas.

NURSEHOUND and SMALLSPOTTED CATSHARK
(Scyliorhinus stellaris, Scyliorhinus canicula)

The Nursehound Shark is also known as the Bullhuss and the Huss and while the name doesn't sound very sharky this 1.5 metre (4 ft 6 ins) shark is a handsome creature. Large spots and dots cover a creamy golden brown topside. The Nursehound inhabits waters all round Britain's coasts and egg cases or mermaids' purses found washed up on the shore may have contained baby Nursehounds that take around nine months to hatch. This shark has no real commercial value and so is not targeted by fisheries. Nevertheless, the Nursehound is on the IUCN Red List as "near threatened". It eats cephalopods, crustaceans, molluscs, bony fish and small sharks.

Confusingly, the really pretty little Smallspotted Catshark is also known as the Lesser Spotted Dogfish. Reaching lengths of up to 50 cms this is our smallest commonly sighted shark. Like the Spurdog, the Nursehounds are a favourite among aquaria, where they do really well and frequently breed in captivity. Often taken as by-catch in fisheries, the Smallspotted Catshark has a high survival rate when discarded and returned to the sea. Of all our sharks, this species is possibly the least threatened and the population is thought to be stable. Crustaceans, gastropods, small bottom invertebrates, worms and fish are all on its menu.

Chapter Seven

WARM BLOODED HUNTERS
THE BIG THREE:
MAKOS, PORBEAGLES AND THRESHERS

SHORTFIN MAKO (Isurus oxyrinchus)

Highly valued by anglers, the Mako is the fastest shark, a real fighter and, some say, the most intelligent.

There are records of Makos in all British seas but in recent years there have been few confirmed sightings. If we take West of England shark fishing activity from Dorset round the peninsula to Somerset, I would estimate that more than 100 angling boats chum for sharks each summer. Over a three-month period each year that's a lot of water covered by a lot of chum, and, if Makos were there, we would be hearing of encounters. Canadian research for the western side of the Atlantic shows the Mako to be seriously depleted, and anecdotal evidence from British seas indicates the same.

The record for a Mako caught in British waters is held by Mrs. J Yallop for a shark caught on May 12th 1971. It weighed 227 kgs (500 lbs). (See page 30)

Like its cousin the Porbeagle, the Mako – whose name is derived from the Maori for shark - is good to eat and it is this, together with its noted fighting abilities, that make it the most prized of sharks by big game anglers. Makos breach (jump) when caught on rod and line. Indeed, a series of athletic leaps is common. The Shortfin Mako has long been a recognised species in British waters, unlike the Longfin Mako. Cornish angling skippers believe the Mako is the most intelligent shark and, while this opinion is based on anecdotal evidence, it is a fact that the Mako does have the biggest brain of any shark relative to its body weight.

Craig Thorburn carried out interesting work with Makos in New Zealand. This showed that they learnt to associate some shapes with food. Thorburn's experiments involved black circles and squares. The squares yielded a model fish as a reward while the circles resulted in real fish. The Makos quickly learned to differentiate.

Further work with protective electric fields showed that Makos circled at the edge if they could see a potential meal inside the field. With other sharks the response was to flee to escape the electric field, whereas the Makos' brain overrode this tendency having received the visual information.

Like its cousins, Porbeagles and Great Whites, Makos have equal tails, which means that the upper and lower lobes are of similar size. Also, like the other two, Makos maintain a body temperature higher than that of the surrounding water.

Some shark species have fascinating migratory stories to tell and the Mako is one of them. It is present throughout the world's temperate and tropical seas. However, an American tagging programme revealed that the Mako has a strong preference for water temperatures in the range 17–22 C, and this factor largely determines its travel patterns.

In 1978, Frank Carey attached sonic transmitters to a shark caught off Cape Canaveral. The animal was tracked across the Gulf Stream to an area approximately 100 miles north of the Bahamas. The tag indicated that it had spent most of its time in the thermal corridor it favoured - i.e, 17–22 C. British waters rarely reach summer highs of much above 17 degrees so, in that sense, our seas are at the lower edge of the Mako's apparent preference.

The first evidence that Makos undertake transatlantic travel began to emerge in the late 1970's/early 1980's, when sharks tagged in the Western Atlantic regularly turned up as recaptures on the eastern side. One tagged in the Gulf of Maine was recaptured in mid-ocean 500 miles west of the Azores. In 1984 another tagged off

Porbeagle Shark. © Shark Conservation Society (Allen)

November 2007. 510kg (1122lbs) 5 metre world record Thresher Shark caught off Lands End.
© Rory Goodall

November 2007. 510kg (1122lbs) 5metre world record Thresher Shark caught off Lands End.
© Rory Goodall

Nantucket was recaptured nine months later to the west of Lisbon. Then, in 1992, one was caught off Madeira, having been tagged 11 months earlier 1,600 miles west at Flemish Cap. It appears that they may follow a North Atlantic migration route broadly similar to that of Blue Sharks.

Makos are generally assumed to be fish eaters and this was largely confirmed by a study carried out between 1972 and 1978, when 237 had their stomach contents analysed. Blue fish, tuna and mackerel were the most common remains identified. Squid - a common prey for Makos hunting in deeper water – together with cod and silver hake were also present. Eye witness accounts from around Britain tell of Makos preying on small seals, and a specimen from the Indian Ocean was found to have two turtle heads in its stomach. There are many accounts of clashes between Makos and Swordfish and it is not uncommon to find Makos washed up dead on beaches with Swordfish bills imbedded in them. A large female caught off Montauk in 1977 was found to have a 36-kilo piece of Swordfish in her stomach. The likely size of the whole Swordfish would have been between 180 and 220 kilos.

Makos commonly produce 10 to 15 pups, which are fully developed at birth, and Makos are currently listed on the IUCN (World Conservation Union) Red List as "vulnerable". Females are known to achieve more than four metres in length, while males usually stop short of three metres.

While they are listed as dangerous and may attack if provoked, the International Shark Attack File records less than 50 Mako attacks in the whole world since records began. However, in late November/early December 2010 there were a series of shark attacks in shallow waters off beaches in Sharm el Sheikh in Egypt. There were five attacks and the investigating experts concluded that they were carried out by two species – Oceanic Whitetip and Shortfin Mako. The attacks left one woman dead and three people seriously injured. The Oceanic Whitetip was thought to be responsible for the death and two of the attacks, with the Mako being responsible for the other two.

THE PORBEAGLE SHARK (Lamna nasus)

Sitting at my desk in my office in Bude, North Cornwall, I look straight out to sea. Through my window I can see the place that we catch and tag Porbeagle Sharks. It may come across in this chapter that I look at Porbeagles in an almost proprietorial manner. That is because I regard them as my friends and I am proud that I have contributed to raising public awareness about these amazing creatures and the threats they face.

I started cage diving with Blue Sharks as a tourist activity in Britain in the summer of 2006. I had really hoped to be able to get Porbeagles up to cages as I had done with the Blues, but these are very different sharks to try to attract to cages or to get into the water with. They are fast and wary. Those who have cage dived with Blue or Great White Sharks will have noticed the relaxed, almost laid back way those sharks cruise around the cages. There is nothing relaxed or laid back about Porbeagles. They are swift and dart in and out from the object that has interested them behaving more like Makos than Blue sharks. Close interaction is difficult to engineer; they simply don't appear to like being too close to humans in the water.

The Porbeagle is not a shark that we know a great deal about, so between 14 and 20 July in the summer of 2007 I ran the first ever Porbeagle shark expedition in UK waters, aided by seven volunteers. The aims of the expedition were as below, and a full report starts on page 122.

- To be the first to deploy satellite (pop-off) tags on Porbeagles this side of the Atlantic. Four of the five satellite tags to be deployed were supplied by Nick Pade, a PhD student at Aberdeen University doing his thesis on Porbeagles. I provided the fifth tag.
- To achieve the first decent quality underwater footage and still images of Porbeagles.
- To observe the sharks on the surface and work out how to get cage divers into the water with them.

The precise locations we worked were not published because the sharks would be an easy target for commercial fishermen. Such fears were well founded because the week after our expedition we got reports of a longliner working around Lundy having caught and killed more than 80 sharks; we later discovered the number was closer to 90. During our five days we observed a sex bias towards females of probably 70 per cent. So the catching of nearly 100 sharks, mostly females, will have had a devastating effect.

I knew that obtaining underwater images, both still and moving, would be difficult due to the Porbeagles' nervousness. Twice previously I had Porbeagles around my RIB in chummed situations and tried to slip into the water to get shots. On one occasion, I dropped into the water on the opposite side of the boat to the shark, but, by the time I had sneaked round the back hoping for a shot, it was gone. On the other occasion I repeated the tactic with only slightly more success. The shark did a fast, crossing pass angling towards me but jinked away just as I was thinking a shot might be possible. Therefore, I reckoned that the best chance of getting images lay in doing so by remote means. Simon Spear was the expedition's videographer and, using a polecam, assisted by Mike Sharland and David Green with a back-up camera, he obtained good footage on day one. We had five different sharks round our boat that day and, as soon as we had one in the chummed area, it would find the bait tube. Thereafter, I would work the shark towards the boat by using the tube. This was how we got the sharks close to the polecam for the movie images and from that footage we ran off still images.

The original plan was to catch sharks for tagging at the beginning of the expedition and then move on to the more difficult task of photography. As it turned out, the difficult part was achieved first! During the next four days we deployed four out of five of our satellite tags, three return tags, and took fin tips for DNA analysis. One tag was set for 30 days, two tags for 60 days, and the other for 90 days. The 30-day tag popped up on time 67 kilometres away off Newquay, the second 60-day tag surfaced near Lundy and the third, 170 kilometres south west of Land's End. The fourth, the 90-day tag re-surfaced 200 kilometres west of Ireland heading out into the Atlantic.

 It's rare that you get to tick all the boxes. We deployed our tags, got our images, collected DNA and, during the video and photographic part of the week, I had an excellent opportunity to study the sharks free swimming near the boat.

From what I had observed cage diving was a problem well worth attempting to crack because these sharks would be really exciting to view. They are reactive to chum. At one time, I thought they were darting in and buzzing the pole camera, and then I realised the camera was right beside the chum bag. The mirrored bait tube had proved a very successful tool with Blue Sharks and so it was with Porbeagles. They never tried to grab it but always checked it out giving me hope that we could use it to work them up to a cage. As stated in Chapter 5, the main reason for caging is to keep all humans involved under control in one place. Deploying the cage over the side from the time of arrival and at the start of chumming would mean that the sharks approached seeing the cage as part of the boat's profile. As I said on page 59 sea conditions and the weather really limit the development of shark eco-tourism off Cornwall. In the four summers since 2007 we haven't had good conditions and sharks at the same time. I am convinced that people would come from all over the world to dive/swim with Porbeagles, but at the moment our great British summers continue to ensure they are left alone.

Porbeagles school (or form aggregations), which makes them very vulnerable to over angling or over exploitation by commercial fishing. There are many examples of this. One occurred in December 2003, when Newlyn-based fisherman Martin Ellis caught and killed more than 130 Porbeagles in a week off South Cornwall. As already stated, another occurred a week after the end of our expedition, when a

Bideford-based longliner caught over 80 sharks in a single day near Lundy Island, which is 12 miles across the water from where we were working.

In 2007 our chumming activities had produced as many as 10 sharks around the boat at one time, so this was first-hand experience of how easy they would be to catch in large numbers once they had formed groups.

Research from the Western Atlantic indicates that Porbeagles often hunt together in loose groups of 20 or more. It is not established that Porbeagles hunt cooperatively but in his book "The Private Lives of Sharks" Michael Bright describes occasions when small groups of Porbeagles have been seen to herd prey into tight balls, with each shark taking its turn to charge into the ball and feed.

Like the Mako, the Porbeagle is warm-blooded, which enables fast pursuit of prey. Mackerel, Tope, Dogfish, Squid, Cod, Herring, Hake, Haddock and others are all on the menu. I am not aware of any hard evidence of Porbeagles taking mammalian flesh, but have heard claims from Cornish and Scottish fishermen that small seals and cetaceans (porpoises, dolphins) are also part of their diet. Certainly, they are opportunistic feeders and I can see no reason why a small, sick seal pup, porpoise or dolphin would be passed up as a potential meal.

The world angling record - a 230 kgs (507 lbs) Porbeagle was caught in British waters in 1993 in the Pentland Firth by Chris Bennett (See page 34). In common with most of the other really large Porbeagles caught around Britain, it was a female. I have encountered several females of more than 200 kilos and up to three metres in length, but have only ever seen one male specimen that approached the 200-kilo mark.

THE THRESHER SHARK (Alopias vulpinus)

On 27 September 2007, I received a text message from Phil Britts on board his boat, the Blue Fox, fishing near Trevose Head, in Cornwall, saying that he had just seen a four-to-four-and-a-half metre Thresher swimming near him. I have never seen a live Thresher in British waters, so I was immediately envious. The only Thresher I have seen in the UK was a dead female awaiting auction in Looe fish market in 2002. Truly a sad fate for a once magnificent animal.

Two months later (21st November) I received another call about an even larger shark, which, in fact, turned out to be a world record. This female Thresher was caught by accident by Roger Nowell while fishing for squid off Land's End. This giant weighing a colossal 510 kilos measured five metres in the body, and around

10 metres when the length of the upper caudal (tail) fin was added. It got caught in the boat's nets and, despite being alive, it was not judged possible for it to be released and to survive. Roger explained: "We'd only been out a few minutes and we brought the net up to have a look. There was no squid but this massive shark – it was the biggest one I'd ever seen. It was fairly alarming. It was still alive but had almost drowned in the nets and, as soon as it landed on deck, it thrashed around like crazy. It caused around £500 worth of damage to the hydraulics, it was that heavy."

I asked my friend and colleague Rory Goodall, of Penzance, to get me pictures of the shark for this book. (See pages 78-79) Later, this magnificent creature made a pitiful £0.23p per half kilo when sold at auction at Newlyn fish market. Prior to this new world record the largest Thresher previously recorded was a specimen caught off New Zealand in 1981, which weighed 363 kilos - just the difference in weight between the two is the size of a large shark.

The Shark Conservation Society (SCS) has compiled a UK Thresher Shark database which will be published early in 2012. The database makes clear that while not abundant, Threshers can certainly be considered a commonly occurring British species. In the last 50 years there have been over 100 confirmed sightings in our waters. The mid Channel and especially round the Isle of Wight is something of a hotspot with anglers reporting catching up to 20 sharks annually. The database starts in the early 1800's and lists over 130 sightings. The authors of the SCS report confirm that new sightings are coming to light all the time, so the figures mentioned here are certain to increase.

Danny Vokins is a well known Isle of Wight-based shark angler. Down the years he has caught Blues, Porbeagles and now his main target species is the Thresher. The British record rod-and-line-caught Thresher is a 146-kilo specimen caught off Gosport by Steve Mills. In 2007, Danny caught one he estimated at more than 227 kilos. But, as Danny tags and releases all his sharks, his potential record was released and swam away.

I have never been sure what constitutes a shark attack because there are variations in the way the word "attack" is used. Bumps or nudges can count as "attacks" to some but in my book they don't. Danny Vokins and Ross Staplehurst felt "attacked" in June 1981, when at 2.00 pm a 181-kilo Thresher jumped into their boat, the incident making headlines around the world. Danny and Ross were saddened that, together with the others on board, they couldn't lift the large shark to get it back overboard and into the sea. They had to kill it and take it back to shore. (See chapter 8 page 97)

Threshers have been caught around the Isle of Wight in small numbers for as long as Danny can remember. In 2002, however, the numbers rose to the 20 previously mentioned.   In recent years there have been reliable accounts of Threshers appearing all round the British Isles. They are distinguished by having huge tails that are almost the same length as their bodies. In nature, everything exists for a reason and so the Thresher's giant tail must serve a purpose.

Also known as the Thrasher, Fox Tail, Fox Shark, Whip Tail and Swivel Tail, the Thresher's names probably come from the many stories of sharks using their tails to secure prey. Accounts of the tail being used to disable fish, thrashing and stunning them, and being used as a herding device to pack fish together prior to devouring them are legion. In 2010 the first footage was obtained which recorded Threshers using their tails to stun and collect their prey together, so the theories were proven to be fact. There are also stories of a man being decapitated by a Thresher's tail, and of seabirds being struck on the surface and then eaten. What is certain is that the Thresher's tail is a formidable weapon.

Of the three species of Thresher - the Pelagic Thresher, the Big Eye Thresher and the Thresher itself - only the latter is commonly found in British seas.Threshers produce litters of between two and six pups, which, like their warm-blooded cousins the Mako and the Porbeagle, feed in utero off unfertilised eggs.

Finally, and regrettably, the Thresher is on the IUCN Red List, is very vulnerable to fisheries and thought likely to be highly depleted.

Cartoon Chris Wylie.

Chapter Eight

SHARK ATTACKS

Despite all popular perception, there has never been a "real" shark attack involving serious injury to humans in British waters. But the "Jaws" fear persists: razor sharp teeth tearing into human flesh while the victim thrashes helplessly around and the water turns red...etc! As I said at the beginning of Chapter I, I believe that sharks hit three basic human fear buttons: being eaten alive, the unknown, and not being in one's own element. Hippos kill many more humans each year than sharks do. But the thought of a "Hippo attack" doesn't send a shiver down the spine; unless, perhaps, at the time you happen to be in a small boat near a large, unhappy hippo!

What follows is a selection of stories from my 2010 book 'Shark Attack Britain'. This book used the stories and photos from the film 'Shark Attack Britain' which I made with my friend John Boyle of Shark Bay Films in 2009/10. Many of the stories are lifted straight out of that book and refer to the film.

DEATH BY DROWNING

Growing to 10 metres in length and weighing the same as a single decker bus, the plankton-eating Basing Shark is generally thought to be harmless. It is the second largest fish in the ocean and now has protection in British waters, which appears to be allowing numbers to recover.

It has always seemed ironic to me that in the early 21st century we know virtually nothing about an enormous creature living on our own planet, and yet we put men into space in the 1960's. Over fifty years since men walked on the moon and we have only now discovered that British Basking Sharks don't hibernate on the ocean floor during the winter, and that they make trans-Atlantic migrations!

The first human deaths caused by sharks in British waters, occurred off Carradale in western Scotland in the Kilbrannon Sound over seventy years ago, in September 1937.

Basking Sharks were much more plentiful than they are now; indeed Basking Shark hunting only stopped in western Scotland in the 1950's. In those days if you looked across from Carradale to the peaks of Arran you would regularly see large numbers of Basking Sharks fins.

I first came across the 'Carradale' incident when I was researching this book.

Next to Carradale is Port Righ which is a small sheltered inlet facing east. Chrystal Patterson is the closest living relative of one of the survivors and of two of those who died, and together with her husband Archie, a one time Basking Shark harpoon gunner, lives between Carradale and Port Righ.

"Chrystal and Archie Patterson being interviewed."

Captain Angus Brown, Chrystal's uncle, was originally from Carradale but had moved to Swansea. Captain Brown and his family used to return to Carradale for their summer holidays. His brothers Robert and Archibald had stayed in Carradale and were fishermen. Their largest boat was the 15 foot Eagle which could either be rowed or sailed. Donald MacDonald was a 14 year old local boy who worked for Robert Brown during the holidays.

There had been a few days of stormy weather, but on Wednesday September 1st the weather and sea conditions improved. It was overcast with sunny spells, there was only a little wind but there were still swells from the south. There were a lot of Basking Sharks in the Sound and many of them were seen breaching (jumping clear of the water). Angus and Robert Brown took the children, Jessica and Neil, out sailing in the Eagle, and young Donald MacDonald went with them. Angus, Jessica and Neil were sitting in the stern, Donald MacDonald was amidships with the oars, and Robert Brown was in the bows.

The little Eagle had her sail up and was making good speed out of the bay when the main halyard snapped and the sail came down. The two men took the oars and started rowing back towards Port Righ.

Suddenly the boat seemed to lift out of the water, there was a splash and then the Eagle was on her side with her mast at an acute angle. Donald MacDonald said that he found himself 9 or 10 feet under the water with the others. Robert and Angus righted the boat and put Jessica and Neil into it. Then the shark which had capsized the boat came back and did it again – there are accounts which say the boat was capsized three times. Jessica and Donald clung to the hull and tried to drag Angus onto it, but he died while they were holding onto him.

The incident had been seen by many ashore and several boats sped to the rescue. Jessica and Donald survived but Robert, Angus and Neil all drowned, Robert's body not being recovered for several days. Newspaper reports suggested the boat had been holed and the attacks were deliberate. Donald MacDonald remembers the hull was 'bruised and marked' but intact. There is no doubt that the Eagle was capsized by a Basking Shark breaching underneath her; equally there is little doubt that this was a tragic accident and not a deliberate attack.

Basking Sharks are thought to breach as part of mating displays and to rid themselves of parasites. Sharks had been seen breaching all morning on that fateful day. Should an animal as large as a Basking Shark decide to charge and attack a little boat like the *Eagle* it would cause very considerable damage. That the *Eagle* appears to have only been struck a glancing blow further supports its having been an accident.

At the time of the incident the *Eagle* was in 26 metres of water which is deep enough for a shark to breach. Donald MacDonald remembers that the boat seemed to stand right up on her end, which suggests a strike from underneath by a breaching shark.

Another theory is that one of the oars may have touched the shark and caused a tail flick which overturned the boat. It's possible but at odds with Donald's 'standing on it's end' statement. We will never know exactly what happened but the best guess has to be that the first capsize was caused by a breaching shark, and the subsequent overturnings may have been tail flicks from the stunned and disorientated animal. One of the rescuers reported that when he arrived on the scene the shark was still at the surface going round the boat lashing its tail. This further indicates that the animal may have been injured by its encounter with the *Eagle*. Chrystal Patterson is the cousin of Jessica Brown who survived. Chrystal Patterson in her interview for the film *Shark Attack Britain* described the incident as follows.

"There were five people in the boat, my uncle Robert, Uncle Angi, my cousin Jessica, my wee cousin Neil, and local man Donald McDonald. They went out fishing which was the big treat when they came on holiday. They were just off the point at the end of the bay and the shark came at them. It jumped below the boat and upset the boat. Uncle Angi and Uncle Robert put wee Neil back in the boat, and Jessica and Donald McDonald. But the shark came back a second time and upset the boat again, they weren't so lucky that time. Uncle Angi was drowned, Uncle Robert was drowned and wee Neil was drowned too. Jessica and Donald McDonald were saved."

A sinister theory that was widely discussed at the time was that this was the deliberate action of a rogue Basking Shark. This is unlikely but there were incidents following the Eagle tragedy which at the time fuelled and supported the rogue shark theory.

A few days after the Carradale tragedy the *Lady Charlotte*, which was a Campbeltown fishing vessel, was returning home from Arran laden with herring. A member of the crew standing at the stern saw a large shark charge at the boat. The shark struck the propeller a glancing blow. The stern of the boat was lifted 3 feet out of the water by the impact and came down again with a crash, fortunately on an even keel.

Some days later a passenger steamer called the *Dalriada* was coming into Carradale. There was a large number of sharks on the surface which submerged as the steamer came in. One shark however stayed on the surface and made straight for the ship. The animal circled the *Dalriada*, leaping out of the water and lashing its tail. The shark did not attack the ship, but there was a theory held by the locals that this was the same shark responsible for the *Eagle* tragedy. It was claimed that they could identify this shark because it was aggressive and larger than most of the other sharks.

"The graveyard near Carradale".

I believe we can safely discount the rogue shark theory and any idea that this was a deliberate 'attack'. I have spent many hours on and in the water off Cornwall watching Baskers and swimming with them. Breaching sharks are a familiar sight to me, and I can readily imagine the scene as a shark came up underneath the *Eagle* and overturned her. I believe the Carradale incident was a tragic long odds accident.

Shark Suicide Bomber

The West Briton and Royal Cornwall Gazette dated August 2nd 1956 contains an account of a coroner's inquest at Falmouth. This investigated how two Royal Naval men were severely injured, and two civilians killed, when an attempt to kill a shark by using explosives went tragically wrong.

Lt. Commander J.W. Bailey explained to the coroner Mr L.J. Carlyon what had happened when he was in charge of a team of divers working off Porthkerris Point. His colleague Lt. Commander Brooks was working on *HMS Burly* while the divers were operating from a smaller fishing vessel manned by civilians.

Two divers were under water while a third was swimming on the surface. Brooks

"My investigations into this incident started at the offices of the West Briton".

saw a shark approaching which he judged to be a dangerous animal rather than the 'harmless' Basking Sharks that were commonly encountered. Brooks stated that he had experience of sharks in America, so presumably his judgement that this was a dangerous shark was based on that experience.

He saw the shark swim towards the man on the surface. **The West Briton** newspaper reports 'As it made its run in it turned on its side, which the witness understood was to get its mouth in position to attack. As it came up to the person on the surface, who was unaware of its approach, bubbles came up from one of the divers below. This frightened the shark which broke off its attack and went away'.

The next day at 1.15 p.m. the *Burly* was back in the same place and so was the supporting fishing vessel. *Burly* signalled the fishing vessel that diving should commence and the divers began putting on their gear. As the divers were preparing, Lt. Commander Brooks noticed a shark circling the fishing vessel.

The events of the day before were still fresh in everyone's minds and Brooks sensed there was some anxiety about making the dive.

"*The author and Charles Hood re-enacting the incident for the film 'Shark Attack Britain'* ".

(N.B. Although I believe it is highly likely that the shark/s concerned were in fact Basking Sharks we must remember that Brooks and his men were convinced this was a predator 'dangerous to man'. It is not spelt out anywhere but one gets the feeling that they thought the shark was a Great White. The events that followed must be viewed in the context that those on the spot were convinced they were dealing with a dangerous animal.)

There was a dinghy moored astern of the fishing vessel and the civilians Leslie Nye and his friend Richard Kirkby together with Lt. Commander Brooks jumped into the dinghy and set off after the shark with the intention of destroying it. Brooks apparently felt that it was his duty to do this to ensure the safety of his men as he was convinced that the day before the shark had been about to attack the man on the surface.

The account in the West Briton continues...... 'As far as we can tell at this stage they got themselves right up close to the shark which was near the surface and swimming away from them. They had made two charges to straddle the shark, and together Brooks and Spicer threw them at the shark. It was a very good shot. A line linking the two charges straddled the shark and got around either its dorsal fin or its tail. The two charges were hanging either side of the shark with the fuses burning. The boat

started to turn away from the shark, but the shark turned around and made for the boat, and was underneath, directly aft, when the two charges exploded'.
(N.B. This is the first time in the newspaper account that we hear of the man named Spicer who was also aboard the dinghy.)

The explosion killed the two civilians Leslie Nye and Richard Kirkby, and the two Royal Naval men, Lt. Commander Brooks and Petty Officer Spicer, were both seriously injured.

The estimated time between the fuses being lit and the explosion was 10-12 seconds, and the explosive was 14 ounces of T.N.T. The court examined whether Brooks had used the right amount of explosive and whether his actions had been appropriate. Lt. Commander Bailey was in the wardroom of the *Burly* having lunch at the time of the explosion. He told the court that he had been told nothing about the dangerous shark being in the area, and thought that diving operations were proceeding as normal. He heard two explosions very close together and thought it was an emergency signal. He went straight on deck where a sailor said "There is a small boat just blown up".'

The small fishing vessel rushed to where the explosion had occurred and was later jointed by *HMS Burly*, which had been at anchor and taken longer to get under way.

As soon as the fishing vessel reached the accident location five men leapt into the water to assist survivors. The bodies were taken aboard the fishing boat which steamed at speed to Porthkerris steps. An eye witness said that the dinghy had been "absolutely smashed to pieces" and he didn't see any sign of the shark.

The coroner commented that it had turned out to be a rather costly experiment. To which Lt. Commander Bailey replied *"The whole question of dealing with sharks is very difficult. I spoke to Brooks about it and he said he was once in an American submarine which got some wires around its screws, and while he and another diver went over the side the Americans held them off with a machine-gun type of weapon"*

The West Briton continued..... ' Witness said he understood sharks sensed when the prey they were going to attack was frightened and it was going to be an easy kill, and that when they smelt blood they lost all fear. On the previous day the man on the surface probably looked likely prey whereas the men in diving suits would appear strange. He believed it was accepted among divers that if they released a few bubbles and shouted, sharks would go away.'

The coroner asked Lt. Commander Bailey whether he would have permitted the use of explosives had he known they were going to be used. Bailey responded that he would have wanted to be fully briefed but he trusted Brooks and his judgement one hundred percent.

Another witness was Leading Seaman P.H. Alderton who was one of the naval divers aboard the fishing vessel. He told how he and Leading Seaman Lusty were preparing to dive when someone noticed a shark circling their boat. He confirmed that Brooks had identified the shark as a 'dangerous type', and that everyone was slightly nervous about diving. Alderton further confirmed that it had been Brooks' plan to go after the shark and scare it away with the explosives. Alderton told the court of the double explosion and said he turned to see pieces of the dinghy flying through the air about two hundred yards away from them.

A helicopter was despatched from RNAS Culdrose to Porthkerris with naval Doctor Surg. Lt. A C Johanssen aboard. Leslie Nye's death was due to head injuries and Kirkby died of blood loss. It was stated that Lt. Commander Brooks and P.O. Spicer were both still very ill in hospital but were progressing well.

And what of the shark? Was this the first ever shark suicide bomber or did the animal survive? Although Commander Brooks felt this was a predatory shark, I suspect it actually was a Basking Shark. These are large animals and blowing one up would certainly result in a lot of blood and shark debris at the site of the explosion. The fishing vessel was on the spot in minutes and there are no reports of a live, dead or injured shark being seen.

The Basking Sharks I see off Cornwall commonly range between 4 and 6 metres in length. Had this even been a Great White, Mako, or Porbeagle shark of say 2-3 metres, it is still strange there was no evidence if the shark was blown up.

The incident was big news in the area and the explosion occurred quite close to land. So had shark parts been washed up there would certainly have been reports – I have looked and found nothing.

This incident like the one in Carradale some twenty years earlier, was a tragic accident. Unlike Carradale, however, in this case man certainly had a hand in his own destruction.

Two Chefs

If you are in the restaurant business and your name is Smith then statistically as far as shark attacks go you are in a very high-risk group!

"An unusual sight to see in your rear view mirror!"

We've looked at the tragic accident at Carradale and also at the bizarre disaster of the attempt to blow up a shark. Our shark attack trail now traces two really quirky tales of restaurant workers called Smith both being attacked by sharks on land!

The Sunday Times dated 9 September 2001 told the story of **Darren Smith, a chef from Newquay, Cornwall**.

Darren was driving a seven-foot shark to a restaurant. The shark was on a bed of ice in the back of his van. He braked sharply and the 110lb shark shot forward and ended up with its mouth on his shoulder. He reached over to grab the shark's nose and push it back. It seems he missed the nose and ended up with his hand in the shark's mouth. Whether the shark's mouth closed on his wrist, or whether he just caught his wrist on the shark's teeth I don't know. However he suffered a severed artery which would have made the inside of his van a very bloody place to be sitting.

"The nurses at the hospital couldn't stop laughing" he said. "I must be the first person in history to be attacked by a shark on dry land!"

As we will see he wasn't the first and probably won't be the last. Being on dry land in Britain is no guarantee of being safe from shark attacks, in fact statistics show you are safer in the water!

"Richard interviewing chef Paul Smith".

Our second chef shark attack victim was Paul Smith. The Blacktip Reef Shark's usual home is tropical reefs. A landlocked pub in rural Worcestershire would not be where you'd expect to find sharks, and certainly not where you'd expect a shark attack. Miami, the Blacktip, measured 2½ feet and his British residence was a 3,000 gallon aquarium in the Fountain Inn pub near Tenbury Wells. The young Blacktip shared his home with 1½ foot catsharks Forest and Jenny.

Paul was feeding Miami fish bits while his diners watched. Paul wasn't quick enough and the Blacktip grabbed his fingers giving him wounds which required stitching in the nearby hospital. The sharks had smelt the prawns and Paul's blood, and became very excited.

Paul told his story to the Sun newspaper. "They must have got a whiff of the prawns – they shot across the tank like bullets. Within a second the water was churning like the shark attack scenes in the Jaws movie – and my hand was in the middle of it. Miami did the most damage. He was hanging off my finger and I was howling. The nurses thought I was mad when I turned up at the hospital and told them a shark had got me".

Paul's boss, restaurant owner Russell Allen who was a shark fanatic and had installed the 15 foot tank, rushed Paul to hospital. Russell told the Sun, "Diners love watching the sharks at feeding time, it must help them work up an appetite – seafood sales have gone up 40 percent". He added, "Paul was very lucky to have only needed a few stitches".

Too Close For Comfort

An incident occurred off the Isle of Wight in June 1981 which could easily have added to the (thankfully) small tally of human deaths caused by sharks in British waters.

Danny Vokins is a well known shark angler living on the Isle of Wight. On the day of the incident he was out shark fishing on his friend Ross Staplehurst's boat.

They had been chumming all morning, with baited hooks and lines out. They knew there was a shark around. In Danny's words he could almost 'feel' it, and it felt as if the shark was stalking them.

Suddenly, just after 2.00 p.m., a 181 kilo (398 lb) Thresher breached right beside the boat and then a second later landed in the boat with the (more than a little) surprised anglers. The shark was too big and heavy for those aboard to be able to lift back over the side and into the water. It was with great sadness that they had to kill the shark, but it could have been the safest thing to do because the tail on a Thresher that size could kill or seriously injure a human. Hazardous though the tail could have been there is also the little matter of the miracle that no humans were injured when a 28 stone shark landed among them.

"Danny and Ross commented as follows.
Danny: *"We were out fishing a club competition and after about 2 hours we saw a big shark jump about 1/2 a mile from us. 3 or 4 minutes later it jumped again, this time only 300-400 yards away, another couple of minutes went by and it jumped right alongside the boat. It got caught in a fishing line and took off at a rate of knots. Then it jumped again about fifty metres away and a split second later it jumped into the boat. It had been getting closer all the time, almost like it was stalking us. The story got into the press, and went worldwide. We were 5 people in a 25 ft boat with a 14 ft 400 lb shark. Its amazing no-one was hurt or even killed".* Ross: *"The boat lurched right over. It hit the boat so hard it either killed itself or knocked itself out. If we could have put it back in the water we would have, but it was too big to lift and a fish that size could have been very dangerous so we had to kill it for safety's sake."*

As we have seen Thresher Sharks are not uncommon around the Isle of Wight in the summer months and 15-20 sharks are caught, tagged and released in this area each year.

"In the office talking to camera describing the IOW incident (from the film 'Shark Attack Britain')".

"They had a lucky escape, that tail could take your head off (Copyright, Vokins) ".

Danny Vokins and Ross Staplehurst are still Thresher Shark angling around the Isle of Wight and all the sharks they catch are released.

Beesands Mako

Jim Johnson was a member of the Aldershot Dolphins diving club. It was the club's custom to take an annual diving holiday, and in 1971 the site they chose was Beesands in South Devon which they visited in June. The incident described in this chapter took place on June 12th.

After unpacking in his caravan Jim decided to go for a snorkel and took with him his 'lobby' hook in case he saw a crab or a lobster which he could take for supper. He swam out and was about 50 yards from shore in 25-30 feet of water when he found he had company.

In his words as reported in Diver (Triton) magazine: *"All of a sudden there he was! A shark. My shark. The only shark in my life. He looked as big as a bus – a 12 foot long bus that is. Allowing for water magnification he must have been a good 8-10 feet long.*

His first thought was that it was a Basking Shark, his second thought was that Jacques Cousteau's method of repelling sharks was to bang them on the snout with a wooden pole. His thinking got more serious as he realised that this wasn't a Basking Shark but perhaps a dangerous shark."

In his own words Jim was terrified and genuinely believed he was in a situation which threatened his life.
"The shark had swum a little ahead of me, his own head about a foot below the surface. He suddenly turned and came at me fast head-on. Although I had a knife strapped to my leg I had no thoughts of getting it out. I just stuck my 'lobby' hook out, pointed end first.

The hook hit him where you would think his forehead was and he passed closely underneath me and then circled me about five feet away. I could see every detail, his snout, his hungry looking mouth, his tough abrasive skin. He also had a silver coloured remora just below and behind his gill slits.

After what seemed an eternity of circling around me he flicked his tail and shot off into the blue. Panic took complete control of me. I swam madly for the shore with my head down in the water looking out for him. I must have made more commotion than a drowning man or a dying fish for he came back and took up his awful circling again. I just kept finning and hoped for the best.

"On the beach describing the Beesands incident. (from the film 'Shark Attack Britain')".

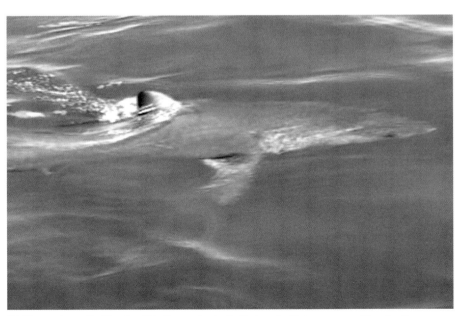

"We'll never know the identity of the Beesands shark - Porbeagle, Mako, or even a Blue shark".

Luckily, I was soon in 10-15 feet of water, and he left me once again. I crawled up on to the beach and collapsed in a state of exhaustion, emotional rather than physical.

A friend, Brian Poulter, came down to me. "Find anything" he asked. When I gabbled out my story he thought I was kidding, but just then a second club member, John Timpany, came running down to us. "Did you see that shark" he said. Did I see that shark! After I told him what happened he said, "I thought you must have seen it because he was so close to you". Quite a comedian is John. After a drink to calm myself I tried to identify the shark with the various fish books owned by club members. As far as I could tell it was either a Porbeagle or a Mako. I go for the Mako because it is the slimmer of the two, and from what I could remember my shark was slim – like a torpedo.

Why didn't he take a lump out of me? I don't know. Apparently so many factors could influence him one way or the other. I was told later by the locals that seals were common the other side of Start Point, so he may have thought I was a seal.

Probably what deterred him from taking any further action was the low water temperature or the smell of my neoprene wet-suit (or me). I like to think that what really stopped him was the thump he got on the head with my 'lobby' hook. Anyway that's my story and I'm sticking to it.

"John Timpany being interviewed on Beesands beech (From the film 'Shark Attack Britain')".

Although a shark was sighted by club members from our boat on two occasions later on during the holiday, he was never again see by divers actually in the water.

There was one poor chap, though, who was given the fright of his life by a black polythene bag at 30 ft!"

The aforegoing section in italics has been reprinted from Diver magazine (then called Triton) and is the copyright of Diver magazine – thank you to Diver.
Porbeagle or Mako? We'll never know but the likelihood is that it was a Porbeagle simply because they are commonly found in our waters while unfortunately Makos are rare.

Jim's fear was totally understandable even though it is more likely that the shark was being curious than attempting to attack him. This incident occurred nearly forty years ago, and in that time our knowledge of sharks and our attitude to them and the threat they pose has changed dramatically.

We interviewed Jim's friend John Timpany for the film and here is what he told us.

"We arrived down here on holiday with my family. It was about late afternoon in June and the weather was beautiful, lovely sunshine, glassy sea, flat calm, and he was snorkelling out there, and I was watching him as I was eating, and then suddenly he was only about 60/70 yards from the beach, and I saw this fin go past. I said to everyone else in the caravan did you see that shark, and they just looked up and said no. No, didn't see it, you must have been imagining it. I was looking again while I was eating and it came back again, a fin went past, it was only visible for a few seconds, but it went past him again from a different direction. And again I said did you see the shark, did you see the shark, and they looked up and said no. By that time Jim Johnson was snorkelling in and we got out of the caravan and walked down to the beach to see if he'd caught anything, and then as soon as he got to the shallow bit and he could stand up, he was blurting out that this shark had molested him and it must have been about 8 to 10 feet long, and it came up close that it bumped into him and he had to push it away with his hand spear. Obviously he got quite flustered, snorkelling back as quickly as he could, and then again it came in from the other direction and he pushed it away again. He was really quite frightened and he was explaining all this to us on the beach, which clarified to the others the fact that I saw it."

– – – – – –

Odd Bites

Mid September 1785 – The Brighton shark

In September 1785 an anonymous letter was sent to the London Morning Herald which described an incident which became known as 'The Brighton Shark', and which was still being talked about a quarter of a century later.

It was unusually warm for September and large numbers of people were paddling on the beach, and swimming in the water. One swimmer was some distance out when he saw a shark fin coming at him very fast. The man swam to shore as quickly as he could and was scrambling up the beach when the pursuing shark launched itself at him, and stranded itself on the beach. An eye witness described the incident as follows.

"A number of people, with hatchets, attacked the fearsome creature and killed it. On opening its stomach, the entire head of a man was found inside it, not otherwise altered than being very soft and pappy….The shark was twelve feet in length from its head to its tail".

The shark was named as a Tiger shark and news of this 'attack' caused widespread alarm and kept people out of the sea.

Note. Given that this report is based on an anonymous letter to a newspaper, and there were no corroborating witnesses or stories, it seems possible that the writer was a hoaxer, or a serious Brighton beer drinker! The only other report of a Tiger shark attack in our waters was of a diver being threatened in July 1968 off Cornwall.

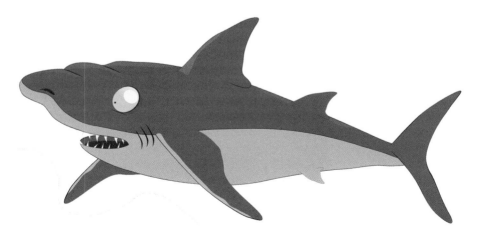

July 1812 – Mill Bay, Devon

It was reported that an unnamed soldier from the Lancashire Militia was swimming in Mill Bay in July 1812 and was attacked and severely wounded in both legs by a shark. The shark was said to have been caught and killed a few days later by local fishermen. Apparently the shark had been eating mackerel and this knowledge suggests that the fishermen cut it open to inspect its stomach contents. If the incident is true the shark is likely to have been a Porbeagle or a Mako.

July 1848 – Hunstanton, Norfolk

"A man was standing waist deep in the sea when he saw something of a most formidable size approaching. He hit out at the creature as he was alarmed, but the animal fought back and struck him with his tail. The animal was a nine foot long shark and a struggle followed which left the shark stranded. Once stranded the shark was killed, apparently the same animal had been behaving aggressively towards bathers earlier that day!"

September 1864 – Granton, Edinburgh

It was reported that a man called Ballard was bitten three times on the leg by a three foot shark. Both man and shark survived, and the shark was further reported to have been seen later in the day by other swimmers.

1876

In his book 'Shark Attacks' Alex MacCormick tells of an incident which occurred in 1876 between Hastings and Fairlight in Sussex. A bather had swum the 400 yards to

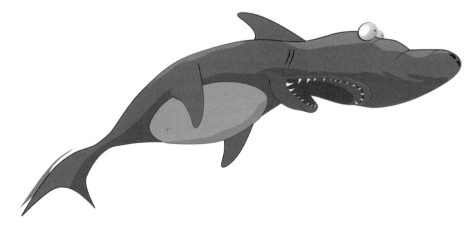

an anchored smack, and on his return swim found himself carried by a strong ebb tide. He felt something come into contact with his left leg and struck at it. He felt his hand rub along a large fish. He yelled out and swam away as fast as he could, but the fish scraped along him another two or three times. He attracted the attention of a nearby fishing boat which came to his rescue. Apparently he almost 'vaulted aboard' in his eagerness to get out of the water.

A large fish was seen swimming around the boat which the report identified as a Blue or Porbeagle shark.

The Times, London, 14 August 1919

"A shark which had made its appearance among women bathers at Croyde, North Devon, on Tuesday was the cause of considerable excitement. The bathers got safely ashore, and the shark was shot by Mr C.C. Cuff, assistant manager in the Great Western locomotive works, Swindon. It took five persons to drag ashore the shark, which measured 7ft 6in in length".

The Times, London 15 July 1924

The paper relates that a twelve-foot shark (unidentified) was caught by fishermen who were netting mackerel. The shark broke two men's arms before it was hauled into the boat.

I would hope that today fishermen would merely cut the shark free and release it thereby not risking either themselves or the shark.

Kent Coast, July 1971

In his book 'Shark Fishing In British Waters' Trevor Housby tells of an 'attack' off the Kent coast when two large Thresher Sharks were said to have attacked a child swimming in very shallow water. Housby states, "I am inclined to think that this attack was more of a chance meeting than a deliberate attempt at man eating". I agree.

The People, London 16 April 1995

"A mother and her three children were treated by ambulance men after inhaling fumes from a dead shark. The one-foot fish, kept in formaldehyde and other toxic chemicals, had been left at their home in Brentford, London".

The Isle of Wight, September 1995

An article in Diver magazine reported a shark encounter 6 miles off the Isle of Wight.

"Wreck diver George Hayward was diving the wreck of the SS Westville with his buddy Trevor Jones. The Westville lies in 40 metres of water. Hayward had an unexpected meeting at around 20 metres. "This shark, of about two metres, brushed against my mask as it went by, I was startled as it passed right against my nose".

No attack, so the pair continued their dive and didn't see the shark again. The diver thought the shark was a Porbeagle which, although common throughout British waters, is rarely sighted by divers. Times have changed: In 1995 this was probably an incident divers would have preferred to avoid, now 16 years later many divers are desperate to get into the water and get close to sharks.

Northern Scotland, June 27 1960

In his book 'Shark Attack' Mac McDiamid records how a young German fisherman, Hans Joachin Schaper was bitten on the arm by a small shark he was removing from a net. Hardly an attack, and such incidents are common, nevertheless this is worth mentioning because the incident is listed as an 'attack' in the International Shark Attack File.

Schaper was aboard the *Mai* and ten days later his wound had gone septic. He was transferred to another East German trawler the *Karl Marx* which landed him at Wick harbour so that he could be given hospital treatment.

– – – – – –

Was he really attacked by the little shark or was this all a communist ploy to put a man on the British mainland into one of our hospitals so that he could spy and steal our medical secrets?! We will never know, but what we do know is that the word 'attack' conjures up all sorts of images, and in British waters the images are almost always the wrong ones.

– – – – – –

So let's examine the four potentially dangerous predatory sharks in our waters in terms of the possibility of an attack. They are the Blue Shark, the Mako, the Porbeagle and the Thresher. According to the ISAF, there have been four recorded Porbeagle attacks globally since records began. The figure for Makos is 46; for Blue Sharks, 38; and for Threshers, five. The ISAF lists three recorded shark attacks in British waters. The first (ISAF 2916 – 1971) is the Jimmy Johnson incident already recounted. The second is ISAF 2296 – 1996. This "attack" involved an unnamed oil rig diver in the Scot Field of the North Sea, who had the mounted light on his helmet "harassed" by a Porbeagle, and the third was the German sailor.

The big three in shark attack terms are the Great White (449 attacks); the Tiger Shark (151); and the Bull Shark (113). The Great White is recorded as being responsible for 79 human deaths, the Tiger for 29, and the Bull for 26. However, these figures must be treated with caution. As George Burgess of ISAF points out, positive identification of the attacking shark is unreliable because, naturally, victims are far more concerned with survival than with the identity of their attacker. Burgess also says that in attacks involving easily identified species such as the Great White, Tiger or Hammerhead, the shark is nearly always identified, while those involved in cases concerning the more-difficult-to-identify species seldom correctly identify the shark. There are those, and I am one of them, who believe that Great Whites are occasional, vagrant visitors to British waters. But there is no serious evidence, anecdotal or otherwise, of Bull Sharks ever being present - the temperature of British seas is outside their normal tolerance range. There have been claimed sightings of Tiger Sharks, but all, so far, are unsubstantiated.

In practical terms, large sharks (those longer than 1.6 metres) can be considered a threat to humans, and it is clear that the two are coming together more often. I have watched the wet suit transform water use in Cornwall. There are now more people using the water and staying out longer all year around. If conditions are good, I can look out of my window in January and see several surfers riding the waves. In mid-winter British sea temperatures are still in the range known to be tolerated by Great White Sharks. Although shark populations are decreasing, human recreational use of the water is increasing, and where humans and sharks interact there is always the chance of an attack. However, even in areas well populated by dangerous sharks, attacks are rare and deaths even rarer. Britain's inshore waters are not well populated by dangerous sharks so the chance of attack is remote. This is well illustrated by the fact that I have been able to find only one record of a witnessed "in the water" shark attack.

In conclusion the term "shark attack" means different things in different places. I believe a fair definition would be that a shark attack is an in the water incident, provoked or unprovoked, when a shark interacts with a human in an aggressive manner with the possibility of injury. Using this definition only one of the recorded "attacks" I have mentioned would be classed as a real attack. Of course shark attacks in British seas are possible but the chances remain remote and the risks tiny. Based on the tales related in this chapter you are in more danger from sharks in British seas on boats or on land than you are in the water. However the Angelshark, Spurdog, Porbeagle and others are all proof that the real danger of 'shark attack' is that of humans killing too many sharks.

Chapter Nine

MY BRITISH SHARK FILMS
(and a BBC Radio 4 Series)

Following publication of the first edition of this book in 2008, I went into partnership with videographer Simon Spear and formed Elasmo Films. Our first project described the events of summer 2007 when we had our tagging and filming success with Porbeagles off north Cornwall. 'Porbeagles in Peril' was a 6 1/2 minute short film shot, edited, and put together by Simon, and I dreamt up the title and did the script and narration. This short film won many awards and we were both very proud of this first collaborative effort.

We had some of the best Porbeagle footage in existence, and Simon had filmed Blue Sharks on trips with me off Cornwall. In theory Threshers, Starry Smoothhounds, Catsharks, Basking Sharks, Soupfin Sharks and others could all be filmed in our waters, and I knew where to find them and who to work with in each location. The idea was born of doing a film based on this book. This led to our forming Elasmo Films, and starting to make plans in the spring of 2009 to shoot "Sharks in British Seas" – the film!

"Sharks in British Seas" (the movie) wasn't big budget, in fact it was no budget. There seemed to be two options – approach a broadcaster and probably be told to make a film involving teeth and gory attacks, or do it ourselves and make the film we wanted to make. We took a deep breath, reviewed our credit cards, prostrated ourselves before our wives and set off.

SHARKS IN BRITISH SEAS

We started work on the banks of the Thames at the London Aquarium on July 1st 2008. We spent the next three days dodging rain showers, town criers, security men, the police and police auxiliaries. We were at the aquarium to illustrate that aquariums are as close as most people get to sharks, and to find out what they thought of the sharks they had seen.

Our first brush with authority came when I was doing a piece to camera outside the aquarium, and an efficient and officious security guard dressed as a town crier asked if we had permission to film there! We didn't but we did have permission to film inside the aquarium, and when we proved this he was somewhat mollified and let us carry on. Later he became very friendly and even offered to do a 'shark' town crying act for us to film. He leapt around shouting and ringing his bell and Simon dutifully filmed his antics. Amazingly Simon somehow lost this sequence when doing the edit! I wonder why?

Inside the aquarium we filmed various sharks through the glass, and from the top of the tanks. We had hoped to get into the tanks to film, but despite the fact that Simon and I have considerably more experience of being in the water with sharks than the aquarium divers, we were not allowed to, and Simon had to hand his camera to them to get the footage for us. Our earlier filming outside had been constantly interrupted by showers, and when we re-emerged the sun was out so we set up to do some shots again, and finish what we hadn't been able to before. We had mollified the town crier security guard, had temporary respite from the rain, but hadn't planned for a lorry drivers' fuel strike. Hundreds of lorries drove slowly through London past the Houses of Parliament intermittently hooting their horns. This circus on the ground was accompanied in the air by helicopters belonging to the police and TV news crews. The almost constant interruption by high levels of intrusive noise made doing 'vox pops' (short interviews) and pieces to camera all but impossible, and to add to our woes the police now took an interest. The Houses of Parliament were very close so there were security considerations, and we were informed that while it's OK for tourists and others to use small handheld cameras and videocams, as soon as tripods and larger shoulder held cameras come out permission is needed. Fair enough, we hadn't known, we should have done, and as we had most of what we needed in the can we headed for Soho to try to get some footage to illustrate the shark fin trade.

On the other side of Shaftesbury Avenue from the arty and sex industry parts of Soho is London's Chinatown. Chinese restaurants and supermarkets crowd together the length of Gerrard Street, with Chinese arches overhead providing further evidence of where you are.

Our earlier brushes with officialdom had made us aware of filming restrictions, and sure enough a couple of police auxiliaries quickly spotted us and we took pre-emptive action and approached them. Simon somehow charmed them and we spent the evening filming in Chinatown at peace with the police.

We found restaurants selling shark fin soup and supermarkets selling fins. As soon as the staff in both places realised where our interest lay they became suspicious and noticeably unfriendly. We did more 'vox pops' on the street trying to get comments that demonstrated the stereotype image that people have of sharks. We also tried to get passersby to tell us what they knew of the fin trade, and discovered that even in Chinatown ignorance among the public of the whole fin trade issue was widespread.

To get footage of all of our sharks would clearly be impossible with the time and resources available, so we concentrated on the ones I have already mentioned which we thought would prove the easiest to film: Blues, Basking Sharks, Threshers, Angelsharks, Houndsharks, Dogfish, Catsharks and Soupfin Sharks (also known as Tope). This was an ambitious shortlist and proved too ambitious during the non-event that was summer 2008; earlier material from 2006-07 came to the rescue.

As any UK diver will know, finding sharks in British waters is no mean feat. This is partly because of the pelagic movements of some of the sharks, the depths at which they live and, the perennial problem of British visibility (assuming you're able to get out to sea in the first place). Of course Basking Sharks can be found close to shore in the summer, but this was far from a classic year for sightings in Cornwall. Blue Sharks were more of a challenge, as they live a long way out and avoid vessels unless there is bait in the water, and as we have seen Porbeagles are skittish and disappear when approached. To film our Porbeagles, we used a variety of techniques involving chumming, teaming up with anglers, and sheer luck. Working on or near the surface, we needed decent light and reasonable sea state. Most of the time we got rain, overcast skies and lumpy water.

As this book demonstrates Britain has a little-known but impressive diversity of sharks. Smooth Hammerheads are infrequent visitors, Shortfin Makos come here more frequently, and it is thought that Blues turn up as soon as the temperature

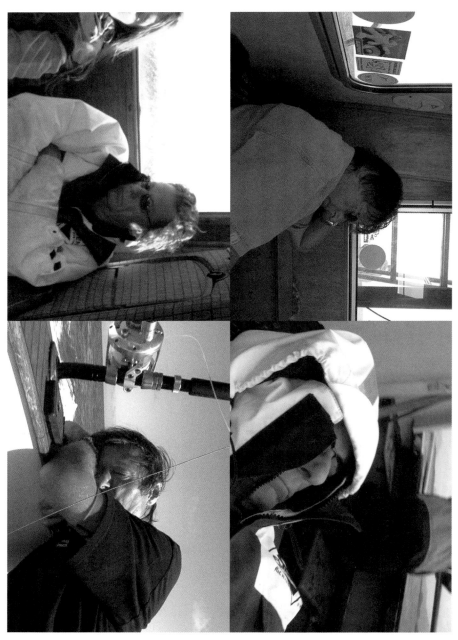

"*Caught napping by Simon Spear. I am really lucky I can sleep virtually anywhere. These shots show that film making is not all action. © Simon Spear*".

Simon Spear in action © Zoe Spear

A soupfin Shark © Simon Spear

goes above 14 'C. Our search for Porbeagles and Basking Sharks took us from Cornwall to the far north of Scotland. Our hunt for Thresher Sharks took us to the Isle of Wight, and the North Sea off Bridlington was the scene of our efforts to film Soupfin (Tope) Sharks. We sought Smallspotted Catsharks in west Wales and Spurdogs in a Highland sea loch.

British sharks are not always easy to find, and they certainly don't want to meet us, but they're out there, and we came across most of them.

Making 'Sharks in British Seas' had been hilarious, challenging, frustrating, hard work and had involved travelling the length and breadth of mainland Britain. The film was a British first and although we were dogged by bad weather, and lacked the resources and budget of big productions both Simon and I were happy with, and proud of, the result.

SHARK ATTACK BRITAIN

I first met John Boyle of Shark Bay Films when we were both trustees of the Shark Trust. John is a multi award winning British underwater film maker, and we started to look for a British shark film to make that would be different and have real impact. I had already done "Sharks in British Seas" with Simon so the normal documentary approach was out.

While researching the first edition of this book and the film I had collected stories of "shark attacks" in British waters. As you will have read in the preceding chapter there has never been a "real" shark attack in British waters, but there have been human deaths caused by sharks, several quirky incidents, and life threatening accidents. We developed the idea of using the British "shark attacks" (or the lack of them) as a way to illustrate the reality of the threat i.e. that sharks were under much greater threat from humans than humans were from sharks. We decided to relate all the shark attack stories I had come across, and then flip the coin over and show the other side of man attacking sharks.

We were really lucky to secure permission from Jed Trewin to use footage he had shot in 2003, when Martin Ellis caught a large number of Porbeagles off south Cornwall. The footage is graphic and horrible and has the impact we wanted. We deliberately chose the eye- catching provocative title "Shark Attack Britain" to attract attention, and did so in the knowledge that most people would buy the film expecting to see one thing, then end up with a different view of the reality of the threat having watched it.

'Sharks in British Seas' had been relatively mishap free, but Simon managed to film me asleep in the wheelhouses of boats in most of Britain's seas (See page 112). 'Shark Attack Britain' provided me with the opportunity to slip on a rock on the Kintyre Peninsula, and end up sitting in a 2 foot deep rock pool to the huge amusement of the film crew who thankfully didn't have a camera running at the time. An hour later, on the site of Anthony Watkins Basking Shark factory, I was trying to do a piece to camera while being eaten by midgets and giggled at by the cameramen who found my discomfort even more funny than my sitting in a rock pool. Two hours later we were interviewing an elderly Scottish woman who was so terrified by the whole thing that she looked as if she were in front of a firing squad. Our attempts to film the harbour in Campbeltown were hampered by rain that belonged in the tropics, and our filming of a thistle to illustrate Scottishness, went fine until my wife told us it wasn't a thistle at all. Just a day in the life of making a film, but a day that I would happily have forgotten most of.

Recreating the Darren Smith in-vehicle attack for the film posed problems. Just where do you find a large predatory shark in England that you can take for a ride in a van? How do you get a dead shark to perform on cue and leap forward to attack its victim? This dead actor has to be prepared to do several takes until the scene has been filmed to the director's satisfaction. Enter Mable, a 7 foot shark caught off Looe by the Shark Angling Club and given to a taxidermist to make immortal. The club gave her to me in a rather dilapidated condition in 2007, but after a hospital visit to my sculptor and modeller friend Scott Gleed, she was restored to her former glory.

Mable isn't any ordinary stuffed dead shark, in fact she is a bit of a media megastar in her own right. She helped me launch the first edition of 'Sharks in British Seas' when she was seen touring north Cornish towns relaxing on the roof of my Subaru. At the same time she appeared in various newspapers and magazines, and has been in front of the camera on many occasions.

Mable rose to the challenge and was taken in a car from her home by the sea in north Cornwall across the peninsula to the Shark Bay film studios in Porthleven, south Cornwall. *(N.B. She doesn't really like riding inside cars and far prefers being on the roof of vehicles in the fresh air. She told me this will be a stipulation in her next film contract!)*

She had to be helped and pushed forward to make her in-car attack on the actor playing Darren, but generally her performance was perfect and is a testament to her acting skills. She drew blood when I got her home – my blood – I caught my finger on one of her teeth when my wife Jacqui and I were putting her back in her cradle in her beach house. Was it deliberate? I'll never know, but I fancy I detected a twinkle in her eye as she watched me suck my finger. Perhaps her acting fee wasn't enough! Making the films was enormous fun, and they all had a job to do which was the reason for making them.

'SHARK HUNT', BBC RADIO 4 SUMMER 2007

There are two wonderful things about doing non live radio programmes – your audience can't see what you are doing, and you can have as many goes as you like to get it right!

In 2007 Martin Kurzik of BBC Radio Wales got a commission from Radio 4 to make a series on sharks found in UK waters. He contacted me to present the series and the first of five programmes was recorded on a day out from Looe hoping to catch and release Blue Sharks. Our skipper was Mally Toms, master of the Jo Dan. Mally is an old friend, a great character and I knew we would have fun whether we caught sharks or not.

During the two hour steam out from Looe, Martin and his wife Barbara did on occasions start to go lighter shades of pale, but both managed to keep the dreaded sea sickness at bay all day. This was quite a feat because the chum (rubby dubby in Cornwall) that Mally produced was as rank as any I had come across in a long time. We bobbed around all day, recorded various background pieces and listened to Mally's anecdotes. When asked by Martin whether he remembered seeing his first shark Mally said yes, it had been many years ago when he was leaning over the side vomiting while suffering from a hangover, and suddenly there was a Blue Shark. Vomit as chum, an interesting idea!

We didn't succeed with our Blue catch but we didn't totally fail either. Mid afternoon we had a take on one of the two rods, and Martin got very excited as he recorded the sound of the reel and Mally and I speculating what we might have hooked. We will never know because the shark dropped the bait before Mally could strike. It had almost certainly been a Blue Shark and at least we'd had contact with a shark on our first day.

_ _ _ _ _ _

Our second foray was off Pembrokeshire aboard the Sabre Tooth II which was based at Nayland Marina near Milford Haven, and operated by Phil and Steve Hambridge. All skippers have good stories, and Steve and Phil didn't disappoint. My favourite was the one that involved Steve being helicoptered to hospital with a hook embedded in the side of his head!

He was unhooking a Blue Shark which they had in-boarded prior to releasing it back over the side. Unknown to Steve the shark had another hook on a piece of line which was wrapped around its tail. An energetic flick of the tail and the hook flew through the air and embedded itself firmly in his temple. Not a hole in the head, a hook in the head, and it had gone deep. If the hook had been in an arm or leg they would have steamed back and taken him to A & E to have it removed. However a hook in the side of the head close to his brain couldn't be touched by them and its removal needed to be done a.s.a.p. They called the emergency services and Steve was winched off Sabre Tooth II and flown to hospital.

The targets for the day were Blues and Porbeagles but we had limited our chances of success before we started, because due to a number of factors we could only work a half day. As with Looe we saw no sharks, but this time we didn't even have a run.

– – – – – –

Danny Vokins boat, Midnight Rambler, is berthed at Bembridge on the Isle of Wight. On August 9th our by now experienced radio crew were steaming out into the Channel in search of Thresher Sharks. So far we'd had a run off Looe but no sharks actually seen or caught. The chum that Mally had used on our day out off Looe had been pretty evil. It was Chanel no. 5 compared to what Danny produced with a sly grin on his face. Blair took us to war looking for weapons of mass destruction in Iraq. He didn't need to go that far, Danny's chum was the smelliest I have ever come across, and soon people were scurrying above or below decks to get out of sniffing range.

Danny's friend Ross Staplehurst deployed his secret weapon, a yellow rubber duck which he used as a float, and we sat back and waited for the duck and the world's smelliest chum to do their work.......and we waited, and we waited, and we waited. Perhaps Thresher Sharks don't like ducks and WMD potency chum because once again we had a blank day in terms of the target species. We did however at last see sharks, as Danny and Ross each caught a Soupfin (Tope) Shark. These were the first sharks that Martin and Barbara had seen, and the day had a successful feel to it even without the Threshers we had hoped for.

– – – – – –

Bridlington in Yorkshire sounds about as 'unsharky' as you can get. This time the target species was Soupfin Sharks and this time off 'unsharky' Yorkshire we got lucky at last. We caught, tagged, and released several of these marvellous sharks. Their taupe colour is what gives them one of their names, and at last I had real shark action to describe for the listeners. I recently listened to this series again and I can hear when I was acting for the benefit of conveying the right effect. I had no need to act on this day; the excitement in my voice is absolutely genuine.

In one sense presenting on TV is easier than on radio. On TV you don't have to describe the place you are in or what's happening around you, the pictures do it for you. On radio the presenter has to paint the pictures in words for the listeners. The danger is getting carried away and going over the top and waxing too lyrical. Our last location was the Pentland Firth. Looking out from Dunnett Head to the Old Man of Hoy on the Orkneys the scene could hardly have been more dramatic. Seabirds wheeled overhead beneath an angry grey sky, the waves crashed into mainland Britain's most northerly point several hundred feet below, and a ridge of water seemed to mark where the Atlantic Ocean met the North Sea. This was a great descriptive opportunity and I had to resist the temptation of over the top presenting. I think I must have found the right balance because I had several phone calls after the programmes aired which picked out this one as my best effort in the series. I certainly really enjoyed doing it.

The waters beneath Dunnett Head are where Chris Bennett had caught his 503lb world record Porbeagle Shark in 1993. In other locations nearby there was just a chance of Common Skate, and so we divided the day into two halves and our anglers set up to try to catch both.

Our port was Scrabster near Thurso and we were aboard the 'Karen' skippered by Davey Benson. Instead of chum (rubby dubby) live cod were being used as bait, and we gave the Porbeagles a good four hours before deciding to move and have a go at Common Skate. It was a good decision because we caught and released a medium sized skate. As with the Soupfin Sharks off Yorkshire the excitement in my voice is audible as I describe the almost ghostly appearance of the 1 ½ metre skate as the angler wound in his line.

The critics liked the shows, the public liked the shows, I had great fun doing them and the pay wasn't bad – win, win and win.

Chapter Ten

THE UK EXPEDITIONS

The first UK expedition in 2003 was conducted under the banner of 'Richard Peirce Shark Conservation'. This was also the case with the first two Adriatic expeditions, the first Cornish Porbeagle expedition, and the 2008 Kuwait expedition. In late 2008 'Richard Peirce Shark Conservation' (RPSC) changed its name and became the 'Shark Conservation Society' (SCS), and after this all expeditions were carried out under the responsibility of Jacqui and myself but in the name of SCS.

CORNWALL AUGUST 2003 – GENERAL SHARK SEARCH

In 2003 the media decided that I would find a Great White Shark off Cornwall. What had started out as a general shark search with a hope that if there was a Great White Shark around we might find it, ended up as a huge international story with me cast as captain Quint!

Of course there were obvious pointers that we were interested in Great Whites – my view that Great Whites are occasional vagrant visitors to our waters is well documented; my friend Craig Ferreira, who is a well known authority on Great White Sharks, came over to help me, and I had chartered the Blue Fox which was the Padstow boat involved in the 1999 North Cornwall shark sighting. Add to this a claim some weeks earlier from a teenager called Chaynee Hodgetts' that she had seen a Great White off Baggy Point in North Devon, and my expedition never had a chance of being anything else than a Great White Shark hunt.

I have had a lot of experience of the media both as a journalist and as the subject of media interest, but I had never personally been the focus of such intense media attention. Before our first day at sea I had done various live national TV chat shows, several local TV and radio interviews, and countless press interviews. When Craig and I arrived in Padstow on our first morning we literally had to force our way through the camera toting throng that were assembled on the steps of the harbour that led down to where Blue Fox waited. I was not really the object of their interest, it was the magic pulling power of the word 'shark'.

What follows is the official report of the expedition taken from our website from which it will be seen that we found very few sharks. The main achievement of the expedition was undoubtedly that it was the biggest shark media event yet to happen in the UK, and as such it provided me with a platform from which to give my conservation message.

It must have worked because for months afterwards complete strangers came up to me in streets all over Britain commenting on what they had learnt about sharks as a result of reading or hearing about the expedition.
NOTE. The expedition reports in this chapter have been reproduced as they were written for the website. I hope this explains the anomalies and seeming contradictions when these reports are read in the context of what happened subsequently.

" EXPEDITION REPORT – CORNWALL AUGUST 2003

From August 6th - 20th 2003 thirteen days of intensive and extensive chumming were carried out on the North Cornish/ North Devon coasts between Trevose Head/Quies Islands and Hartland Point. Fresh and frozen mackerel were used as chum combined with blood and the other materials. Operations were carried out from between half a mile offshore to eight/nine miles out and using tidal currents the whole coast was covered either inshore or offshore.

At the end of the thirteen days only the following sharks had been encountered:-

3 Blue Sharks (Prionace glauca) - 1 male Tope, 2 Porbeagles (Lamna nasus)

5 Bull Huss - 6 Lesser Spotted Dogfish - 8 Basking Sharks (Cetorhinus maximus)

We had expected to encounter a lot more Tope, Blue Sharks and Porbeagles and had hoped for a Mako or Thresher or two and maybe even a Great White. Chumming was conducted on a continual basis in a professional manner and the worrying lack of sharks is a further indicator of the serious depletion in numbers.

The Dalhousie University research produced alarming figures of depletion levels in the North West Atlantic - Hammerheads down 89% - Great Whites down 79% - Tiger Sharks down 65% - Oceanic white tips down 70% - Threshers down 80% and Blues down 60%.

During our thirteen day expedition we worked in a variety of weather conditions in areas which have historically produced sharks. The vessel chartered for the period was the Padstow based Blue Fox which I believe is the last full time professional shark angling boat in operation on the North Cornish Coast.

The Blue Fox crew are therefore highly experienced in finding sharks.

Also on board was Craig Ferreira from South Africa who brought further long experience to the operation.

Given the effort expended and the expertise deployed I am sure that had there been sharks to find we would have found them. In the weeks before the expedition and afterwards until the time of writing I carefully collected and monitored information from recreational shark anglers, longliners and professional fishermen on the same stretch of coastline and the picture was always consistent - no species of shark was being encountered in any numbers.

The Shark Angling Club of Great Britain based in Looe in South Cornwall has kept catch records since the 1960's and the figures for the last ten years are as follows:-

| 1994 = 557 | 1995 = 208 | 1996 = 526 | 1997 = 301 | 1998 = 385 |
| 1999 = 274 | 2000 = 86 | 2001 = 358 | 2002 = 125 | 2003 = 165 |

Compare these figures to the 1960's and 1970's when over 3000 sharks per year was the norm! In twelve specifically targeted trips in 2003 the Blue Fox has caught only two Porbeagle sharks instead of the usual average of 24 in the 1990's. Whilst various factors explain the up and down nature of the figures there is no denying that the trend is down.

The conclusion has to be that the reason we did not find more sharks is that numbers are so depleted the sharks are not there to be found. **//**

CORNWALL 2007 – PORBEAGLE EXPEDITION

The first Porbeagle expedition was my second major UK expedition, and as with the 2003 expedition was conducted under the banner of "Richard Peirce Shark Conservation ". I think of the Porbeagle very much as my shark, and only five years ago a lot less was known about the Porbeagle than is the case today. No-one had tagged Porbeagles on our side of the Atlantic, the public were by and large unaware that we had a first cousin of the Great White resident in our waters, and this critically endangered shark had no protection in British seas. I set out to play my part in changing things.

By the end of the expedition we had ticked all our boxes – I had become the first person to deploy satellite tags on Porbeagles on our side of the Atlantic, we had shot the first free swimming underwater footage of this species, and then a tragic event presented the opportunity to propel these sharks into the national spotlight. We tagged and filmed our sharks just under the cliffs of Morwenstow where GCHQ have a large listening station. Halfway through our expedition one of the Padstow angling skippers told me of a longliner having caught nearly 100 sharks in a morning near Lundy, which was just across the water from where we had been working.

All I had was hearsay, I had no proof. The catching vessel was based at Appledore near Bideford and the catch had been onward shipped on landing. There was nothing illegal about what the catching vessel had done; nevertheless there was a reluctance to talk. I worked closely with a contact who wrote for the Times and he put the story out on the basis of "Conservationists are alarmed at reports that..........." The Times story triggered an investigation by the Western Morning News, and the whole story came out and went national. This was the first major Porbeagle story since the Martin Ellis catch in 2003, and like that story it caught the nation's attention.

Obviously this shark tragedy had not been foreseen when I planned the expedition, but the story became entwined with what the expedition had achieved, and later in the autumn both ITV and the BBC carried Porbeagle stories. There is absolutely no way that I or the expedition can claim credit for the eventual protection that these sharks got under the EU zero Total Allowable Catch (TAC), but I really do believe that we did a lot to put the Porbeagle on the map of British public awareness. The report that follows has been taken from our website.

– – – – – –

" 2007 PORBEAGLE SHARK EXPEDITION - CORNWALL JULY 14 - 19 2007

Personnel and Acknowledgments

Organisers - Richard and Jacqui Peirce

Expedition leader - Richard Peirce

Skipper of Mantis - Karl Bennett

Expedition members / volunteer researchers - Rob Allen, Mark Boothman, David Green, Stuart Patterson, Mike Sharland, Tom Sharland

Videographer / Documentary film maker - Simon Spear

PhD student - Nick Pade (Aberdeen University)

L to R – M Sharland, D Green, T Sharland, Richard Peirce, K Bennett, S Patterson, S Spear, M Boothman

We would like to express: -

- Our thanks to all those who took part
- Our thanks to God for giving us sharks
- Our annoyance and disgust at man's greed in killing them in unsustainable numbers
- Our hope that our findings will not result in the sharks we found being targeted
- Our apologies to the sharks that had to be caught to be satellite tagged for any pain and discomfort caused

OBJECTIVES

The equal joint objectives were research (tagging, abundance assessments, DNA sampling) and movie and still photography.

Underwater still and movie images of Porbeagles are rare to non-existent. The aim is to sell any footage and/or stills obtained to fund a further four years of this project. It is hoped that five years of research will provide ammunition which can then be used to lobby for local protection of Porbeagle sharks with Cornwall Sea Fisheries.

SITES

The expedition decided not to release detailed information relating to capture sites and areas worked. The reason for this is that we do not want to provide a map which will enable commercial fishermen or anglers to accurately target these animals.

One day was lost due to bad weather but the other five days were worked successfully and the sites covered were a large section of Bude Bay between Cambeak Head / Crackington Haven and Knapp's Longpeak.

CHUMMING

Fresh mackerel chopped up and mixed with bran were the chum materials used which were deployed in two chum bags beside the boat (Mantis), and in chum tubes floating on lines up to 12 metres off the stern of the boat.

PERSONNEL / TIMINGS

Richard was joined by seven paying volunteers who are all effectively stakeholders in the expedition and will have shares in any funds received from still and movie image sales. Some members, and Richard and Jacqui, will be putting their shares towards the costs of the next four years of running this project. Nick Pade, a PhD student supervised by Dr. David Simms and Dr. Les Noble provided four satellite tags and Richard Peirce provided a fifth tag. All the data gathered on the expedition was made available to Nick Pade for use in his doctoral thesis.

BOATS

Mantis (8m) skippered by Karl Bennett and supported by RP's RIB Glauca were the two vessels used.

DAILY REPORT

Saturday July 14
Day lost due to adverse weather

Sunday July 15
General area Cambeak Head to Widemouth Bay and off Morwenstow. Size, gender observations, and markings enabled us to positively identify five specimens in the water around both Mantis and the RIB. Good footage using a polecam was obtained of at least four of the sharks and Rob Allen obtained a reasonable still image. No specimens were tagged or fin tipped (DNA) because we were concentrating on filming, and only once did a shark take the bait which was dropped after a short run.

I had expected that free swimming underwater footage would be the most difficult task to accomplish, and so we were all delighted to have perhaps a minute of good footage in the can on the first day.

The mirrored bait tube proved a hugely successful device with all the sharks taking close interest.
In all a total of nine hours chumming were achieved.

Monday July 16
Same general Bude Bay areas as on July 15th. One specimen sighted, a juvenile female caught on mackerel feathers. This animal was tagged with an SAC GB return tag and a tissue sample was taken from the upper caudal.

Tuesday July 17
Day lost due to adverse weather.

Wednesday July 18
Same general Bude Bay area as previous days. Four separate specimens identified, one specimen tagged (PAT) and fin tipped (DNA). The tag was the first satellite tag deployed on the eastern side of the Atlantic on a Porbeagle. The tag was set to pop off in 60 days. The DNA taken was sent to Dr. Mahmood Shivji (USA) and Nick Pade.

Thursday July 19
Same areas worked. Two specimens definitely encountered. One male was return tagged and fin tipped (DNA), the other larger specimen was lost at the side of the boat when the hook came out, the shark swam off strongly and quickly. Interest in baits indicated the presence of more sharks but no further positive identifications could be made.

Friday July 20
Same areas worked. This extra day was added to make up for one of the days lost to weather.

Several sharks were encountered and five were able to be positively identified, a further three satellite tags were deployed set as follows: -

> Female - 90 lb (estimated) - tag set for a 30 day deployment
> Male - 160 lb (estimated) - tag set for a 60 day deployment
> Male - 170 lb (estimated) - tag set for a 90 day deployment.
> DNA (fin tip) samples were taken from all the above (all upper caudal).

CONCLUSIONS / NOTES

It is impossible to be sure of accurate numbers of individuals encountered however I feel it is safe to say that at least twelve separate specimens were encountered in five days and that number could be as high as eighteen or twenty. It was not always possible to sex sharks in the water or to estimate size or weight with reasonable accuracy so we have not attempted to do this.

This was a ground breaking trip which for the first time on this side of the Atlantic deployed satellite tags and obtained good quality footage and still images. We also deployed return tags and took tissue samples. Thus even with the lost day the objectives of the expedition were met.

POP OFF TAG RESULTS
- The first (30 day) tag popped up off Towan Head Newquay, 42 miles from the release site.

- The second (60 day) tag popped off 10km WNW of Lundy Island.
- The third (60 day) tag popped off slightly late 170kms SW of Lands End.
- The fourth (90 day) tag popped off on time 200 kms W of Ireland.

Once the tracks have been established and other data processed a further report will appear on this website. **//**

PORBEAGLE EXPEDITIONS – 2008/2009

The 2007 expedition was by far our most successful. In 2008 and 2009 we tried to mount follow up expeditions but were beaten by unsettled weather. I suppose we had been spoilt on the first expedition and expected similar success subsequently. For the 2007 expedition I had chartered a vessel called 'Mantis' which worked out of Bude, and was skippered by my friend Karl Bennett. Bude is a convenient location for working the two well known Porbeagle grounds at Crackington Haven and under the dishes of Morwenstow. Karl had not been available for the 2008 expedition so I reverted to my long time colleague Phil Britts the Padstow based skipper of Blue Fox with whom I had worked on the 2003 expedition. The problem with using a Padstow based boat for work near Bude is the time it takes everyday to steam up and down to and from the work sites. Working out of Bude you can have chum bags in the water in less than an hour; with Padstow based vessels the time is more than doubled.

As will be seen in the 2008 report that follows (from our website) we had planned seven days and lost three due to bad weather. We steamed to Morwenstow on three days, then on our fourth we had to work near Trevose Head due to stormy northerlies.

// PORBEAGLE SHARK EXPEDITION - CORNWALL JULY 12 - 18 2008

Personnel and Acknowledgements

Organisers - Richard and Jacqui Peirce

Expedition leader - Richard Peirce

Skipper of Blue Fox - Phil Britts

Expedition members/volunteer researchers - Rob Allen, Mark Boothman, David Green, Mike Sharland, Tom Sharland, Simon Spear.

Videographer - Simon Spear

SCS would like to thank:-
- All those who took part
- God for giving us sharks
- Our hope that the data we are gathering will contribute towards meaningful, sensible and workable local conservation policies.

OBJECTIVES

The building of a picture of the local area distribution of Porbeagle sharks at the time of the year of the expedition.

Achieve additional still and moving images to add to the material gathered in 2007.

SITES

The same sites were investigated as in 2007 and for the same reasons will be kept confidential for the time being.

WEATHER

The planned days were July 12 - 18 inclusive. In the event, due to bad weather we lost three days and were only able to work the 13, 14, 15, and 16.

CHUMMING

Fresh and frozen (minced) mackerel were used simultaneously in chum bags and in bait tubes. The chumming materials were totally effective.

BOATS

Mantis (Bude based) was not available this year and so the Blue Fox (Padstow) was chartered for the expedition. The major downside to using a Padstow based boat was the time taken in steaming to the working areas.

DAILY REPORT

Several times sharks appeared at the floats and we tried as quietly as possible to get in the water and sneak out to them. On each occasion the sharks disappeared long before we reached the floats. We would then wait a few minutes and return to the boat, and the sharks would reappear at the floats!

Tagging and releasing Porbeagles © Shark Conservation Society

Tagging and releasing Porbeagles © Shark Conservation Society

Saturday July 12
The wind would have been against us for the whole steam from Padstow to near Bude. Wind speeds 15/20 mph. Cancelled.

Sunday July 13
We were not tagging sharks this year as we planned to concentrate on videography, photography, in water shark/human interaction and local area population mapping. At least three, maybe four Porbeagles around our bait tubes and one likely Soupfin (Tope) Shark also around bait tube. In the same location two weeks before five or six Soupfin sharks on the surface had proved a nuisance to a Porbeagle angling boat which forced the boat to move!

Monday July 14
The same location as the previous day (13 June). Two or three individuals (Porbeagles) around the bait tubes. Water temperatures 16 degrees.

Tuesday July 15
Southern end of our sector. Chummed near Crackington Haven. Two drifts and no Porbeagles encountered.

L to R - Simon Spear, Rob Allen, Mike Sharland, Mark Boothman, Richard Peirce, Tom Sharland, David Green, Phil Britts. © Shark Conservation Society

Wednesday July 16
Strong northerlies made the steam to off Bude impossible so we worked near Trevose Head set up for Porbeagles and Soupfin sharks (Tope). One specimen (Soupfin) caught and return tagged.

Thursday July 17
Cancelled - bad weather.

Friday July 18
Cancelled - bad weather.

OTHER DATES/SITES WORKED BY OTHER BOATS

- 01/06/08. Mantis was angling at the north end of our sector. No sharks were encountered which supports the picture we are building up.
- 25/07/08. Lady Mary was angling at the northern end of our sector - no sharks.
- 26/07/08. Blue Fox was angling at the northern end of our sector - no sharks.

Both the above results support the general picture emerging.

CONCLUSIONS/NOTES

The picture which is emerging supports what north Cornish shark angling skippers have thought for many years. We hope the next three years data gathering will further confirm this position.

SCS is keeping the results confidential so as not to provide a specific information guide for those wishing to catch Porbeagles. The results will be published (grey) at the end of our five year programme.

TAGGING

No electronic tags were deployed directly by the expedition this year. However a tagging effort was made by another group two weeks earlier and reports indicate serious animal welfare considerations. SCS will soon be in discussion with the Home Office seeking reforms to the current rules governing the issuing of tagging licences. We will lobby for reforms which will make animal welfare a prime consideration and will seek that only those with demonstrable relevant field experience should be licenced to electronically tag sharks. **//**

2009 PORBEAGLE EXPEDITION

The 2009 Porbeagle expedition was even more dismal than what we had experienced in 2008. That year we had lost three out of seven planned working days, but in 2009 we lost five out of seven and didn't even see a shark! We got to sea on the first and last days of the planned period and got soaked to the skin on both occasions. Karl was available again so I had chartered Mantis to save us the steaming time from Padstow, but Mantis had engine troubles on the first day so we had to use an open fishing boat skippered by Julian Bolitho.

The expedition members for 2007 and 2008 had been virtually the same. In 2009 we had a chap called Miguel Gallego who had come all the way from Spain to see a Porbeagle, and three new female volunteers who kept smiling all week despite the boredom of being stuck ashore, and the disappointment of not seeing what they had come for.

Volunteers can be good, bad, or indifferent but mostly they are good, and the tolerance and spirit shown by the three girls on the 2009 washout, put them firmly in the 'good' class.

– – – – – –

A Porbeagle investigates the bait tube © Shark Conservation Society

"PORBEAGLE SHARK EXPEDITION - CORNWALL JULY 10 - 16 2009

Personnel and Acknowledgements

Organisers - Richard & Jacqui Peirce

Expedition Leader - Richard Peirce

Expedition members/Volunteer researchers - Abbi Scott, Mark Boothman, Shane Benzie, Miguel Gallego, Rebecca Coales, Simon Spear, Leslie Guinn.

Videographer - Simon Spear

SCS would like to thank:-
- Karl Bennett
- Julian Bolitho
- Marie Glossop (rescue torch holder)

OBJECTIVES

Achieve underwater still Porbeagle images, and underwater film footage.
Determine whether it's possible to cage dive with these sharks.
Continue gathering data for our Porbeagle map of the area.

SITES

Only two sites were worked due to adverse weather. These sites were in the same general area as were worked in 2007/08.

WEATHER

Out of seven days planned only two were actually worked. This was due to an unsettled period of wet and windy weather.

CHUMMING

Fresh and frozen (minced) mackerel in both bags and bait tubes. Chumming conditions were not ideal on either of the two days at sea.

BOATS

July 10th - Lilly May II - J. Bolitho   July 16th - Mantis - K. Bennett

DAILY REPORT

Friday July 10th.
Three sites were chummed across Bude Bay. Conditions were choppy seas, intermittent rain, overcast all day with 15-20 m.p.h. winds. No sharks were seen, but conditions would have made sightings difficult were sharks there. 8 hours worked.

Saturday July 11th.
Cancelled - adverse weather.

Sunday July 12th.
Cancelled - adverse weather.

Monday July 13th.
Cancelled - adverse weather.

Tuesday July 14th.
Cancelled - adverse weather.

Wednesday July 15th.
Cancelled - adverse weather.

Thursday July 16th.
Two sites were chummed at the north end of Bude Bay. Incessant rain all day, choppy seas, 15-20 m.p.h. winds made the sighting of any sharks impossible. 9 hours worked.

CONCLUSION/NOTES

The 2009 Porbeagle expedition was effectively a non event due to weather conditions. Neither of the two days worked produced reliable results due to conditions.
N.B. It has been noted that this is the fourth year when there has been settled weather in May/June followed by unsettled, often unworkable periods during July/August with settled weather returning in September. For our 2010 Porbeagle work we will work on a weather reactive basis and go to sea earlier in June if weather conditions appear settled.

Well done to all those involved for their tolerance and patience displayed during the long boring hours sitting ashore. **//**

// Denotes material taken from the Shark Conservation Society website

L - R: Richard Peirce, Abbi Scott, Simon Spear, Miguel Gallego, Mark Boothman, Rebecca Coales, Karl Bennett, Leslie Guinn. (Absent - Shane Benzie) © Shark Conservation Society

SEPTEMBER 2011 – THE WESTERN ISLES

If one believes, as I do, that Great White Sharks are occasional vagrant visitors to UK waters then it follows there are probably years when no sharks visit our seas, so to mount an expedition specifically to find one would be lunacy. I am not a loony, maybe I'm not totally sane, but I'm not nuts either, so when I've decided to work the areas where there have been credible sightings of Great Whites I did so on the basis of conducting general shark searches for all species rather than specific Great White hunts. In 2003 when I ran the expedition off Cornwall, the press daubed it a Great White hunt. So when we put together an expedition to work in the Western Isles I didn't expect to get away with it there either.

I am quite sure that if I had said to a media interviewer that I had proof positive of the landing on the Hebrides of a green headed alien from Mars and had come to investigate, the interviewer would still have said "Yes, Richard but what about the Great White Shark"?

I always try to have some control of the press by releasing factual news rather than letting them find out that something is going on and then making up the rest. It hadn't worked in Cornwall in 2003 when media coverage went mad and I completely lost control.

For the September 2011 Hebrides expedition it worked. I put out press releases, the media used our information intelligently and for once the coverage, although extensive, stayed within the parameters I had set.

The credible and compelling possible sightings of Great Whites in UK waters are in two clusters which are off Cornwall and Scotland's west coast. A team of ten volunteers including a videographer and a scientific advisor spent between September 16th and October 1st based at Lochmaddy on North Uist with the intention of carrying out the first ever shark survey in that area. The Monach Islands are home to northern Europe's largest colony of Grey seals which start pupping in late September/early October. Where there is prey there are usually predators so the Monachs at the beginning of the pupping season was a logical place to look for large sharks. This tiny group of islands lies seven miles west of North Uist and inside St. Kilda which is the most westerly of the Outer Hebrides. The timing of these expeditions often has to be a compromise between the availability of volunteers (school/uni holidays) and local factors, such as the likely weather and seal pupping together with specific information such as past sightings of species of interest. The timing of this expedition was just such a compromise and I always recognised that the weather was our greatest threat, and the one factor totally beyond our control.

The scientific aims of the expedition were to gather meteorological, oceanic, and other environmental data from the areas around the Monach Islands, through the Sound of Harris and out into the Little Minch, and to conduct a general shark search/survey of the area. Conditions could then be compared to other places in the world where there are known Great White Shark populations and if conditions were, as suspected proven to be identical, then the question of why there isn't a known Great White Shark population, even seasonal, could be addressed. Great White Sharks may never have been plentiful in the north Atlantic and there is no reliable baseline data as to abundance, but they are recorded as having always been present. In the days of whaling activity Great White Sharks were recorded around the Azores; there is a known population on the eastern coast of the United States, and the nearest recorded (proven) Great White Shark occurrence to our shores was a female caught off La Rochelle in 1977. I am convinced there is a high probability that some of the claimed encounters with Great White Sharks that remain credible following investigation did indeed involve these charismatic animals.

So they are in the north Atlantic; we have always known they were there, and in the days before they were so severely depleted why didn't they discover the ideal habitats that exist in some places in the British Isles, and establish resident or seasonal populations? Or did they? Two hundred years ago prior to population depletion would a small number of Great White Sharks around the Monach Islands during the pupping season even have been noticed? Who was there to notice? The Hebrideans would not have been recreational water users, and this was the days before modern industrial fishing? The population in the islands in 1901 was only 46,000, which however was nearly double today's 26,000, so I believe that it is perfectly logical to assume the presence of the sharks could have gone unnoticed.

I raised this point with lifelong local fisherman Willie Stewart. I asked whether large marine predators preying on seal pups from October would have been sure to be noticed. He replied that once the creels had been collected in during October no-one really went there so there was no-one to see anything!

Prior to analysing the data gathered on the expedition Daniel Moore, our scientific advisor, said that it looked as if the general environmental, meteorological and oceanic conditions in the Hebrides, and in South Africa and California are very similar. The full analysis of the data will not be completed until after this book is published, but Daniel's initial view confirms the enigma of why Great White Sharks are not found in British waters.

Both Scottish TV and the BBC wanted to come aboard our vessel and film the expedition. This gives small non-profit societies like the Shark Conservation Society (SCS) a problem in that if a Great White Shark, a Greenland Shark, or anything else unusual turned up and provided the opportunity to acquire unique footage, then we (SCS) would want to shoot it ourselves. The value of the first footage in UK waters of a Great White or Greenland Shark could be thousands of pounds and if such footage were acquired on an SCS expedition by a broadcaster (BBC/ITV) not only would SCS lose the chance to sell it to them, but we wouldn't own the copyright for future sales. The Porbeagle footage shot in 2007 has earned several hundred pounds for SCS, and so obviously these chances have to be kept in-house to avoid shooting ourselves in both feet.

My terms to Scottish TV and the BBC therefore were that in return for a small donation to the Society they could come aboard for a day and film what they liked, but if anything really unusual turned up they would leave us to film it, and would then have to buy the footage from us. Reasonable terms you would think? Wrong, keen though they both were neither could agree to these terms. The incredible selfish arrogance of these large corporations beggars belief. Our volunteers were each paying around £1000 to come on the expedition, and the BBC and Scottish TV not only expected to be able to come aboard for nothing, they then wanted to have the right to rip off a non-profit conservation society! I wonder what colour the sky is in their worlds – pink with purple spots perhaps! I guess the reason is that in general people are so desperate to get their faces on TV or their names in print that they throw all normal considerations out of the window.

The full report of this expedition will be posted on the SCS website once our scientist Daniel Moore has gathered the data referred to earlier. However conclusions will be impossible and the data of limited value, because once again an SCS expedition was all but a disaster due to the weather.

I had planned 14 days work with the Monach Islands as our primary target area, and the Sound of Harris and the east of North Uist as secondary objectives. We only managed six days work at sea and never even got to the Monach Islands. Following this expedition we decided to abandon doing expeditions on pre-planned dates in British waters. Instead we will in future work reactively and put to sea when fair settled weather has set in.

L - R: Daniel Moore, Mark Bradfield, Tim Perkins, Gerald Conway, Richard Peirce, Andy Sweeney
© Thomas (SCS)

L-R J Peirce, S Spear, P Harding, G Conway, L Whitley, R Peirce, M Bradfield, R Coales, A Bennett,
T Perkins, F Sessig, A Sweeney, A Thomas, D Moore, N Ingledew © Peirce (SCS)

Few creatures get the bad press that sharks continue to attract. Cartoon Chris Wylie.

Chapter Eleven

MEDIA FEEDING FRENZIES

Much of what we think about any subject is based on our daily diet of information from the media. Of course, it is much more sensational for sharks to be portrayed as man-eating monsters than victims of over-fishing. The result is that the public is not just badly informed about sharks, it is often completely misled.

Why should it be front-page "news" that Mako Sharks have been seen off the Cornish coast? They have been there for tens of thousands of years. It's not news that a hippopotamus is spotted in a river in Zimbabwe, it's not news that a lion is seen in Kenya or an elephant is seen in India. It's not news because it's normal that they should be there. It's also normal that sharks should be observed in the sea. If a shark was spotted sitting on an aeroplane landing at Newquay Airport that would be news! A shark chasing sheep on Bodmin Moor would be news, but a shark in the sea - where do journalists expect them to be?

This largely pictorial chapter reproduces headlines, images and extracts from articles that have appeared in the UK national press in recent years. I hope that by perusing them as a collection the reader will see what biased, unfair and unbalanced coverage sharks have received. However, perceptions are changing, and some parts of the media now produce balanced, factual coverage. Regrettably, though, many in the tabloid press continue down the "Jaws" road because that's what sells newspapers.

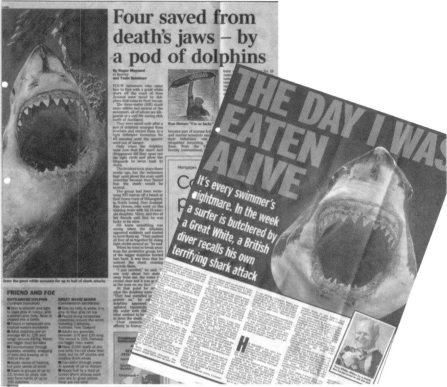

Four saved from death's jaws – by a pod of dolphins

By Roger Maynard
in Sydney
and Tracie Solomon

FOUR swimmers who came face to face with a great white shark off the coast of New Zealand were saved by dolphins that came to their rescue.

The three-metre (10ft) shark came within two metres of the swimmers, all of whom are lifeguards at a surf life-saving club north of Auckland.

They were saved only after a pod of dolphins emerged from nowhere and circled them in a tight defensive formation for 40 minutes until the quartet were out of danger.

Only when the dolphins were sure that the shark had disappeared did they open out the tight circle and allow the lifeguards to swim back to shore.

The incident took place three weeks ago, but the swimmers kept quiet about the story until yesterday because they feared that the shark would be hunted.

The group had been swimming 100 metres off a beach at their home town of Whangarei, in North Island, New Zealand. Rob Howes, who went on the training swim with his 15-year-old daughter Niccy, and two of her friends said that he was lucky to be alive.

He knew something was wrong when the dolphins appeared suddenly and started to herd them up. 'They pushed all four of us together by doing tight circles around us,' he said.

When he tried to break away from the protective group, two of the bigger dolphins 'herded' him back. It was then that he noticed the shark coming towards them.

'I just recoiled,' he said. 'I was only about two metres away from me, the water was crystal clear and it was as clear as the nose on my face.'

At that point he realised what the dolphins were doing. 'They had corralled up to protect us,' he said.

The dolphins apparently circled around the white shark, splashing, repeatedly slapping the water with their tails and doing what seemed to be a dance to deter the shark.

Over centuries the dolphin's ability to human ...

Jaws: the great white accounts for up to half of shark attacks

FRIEND AND FOE

BOTTLENOSE DOLPHIN
(Tursiops truncatus)

■ Skin is smooth and tight to slide glide in water, with a pinkish grey belly. Snout is shaped like a bottle.
■ Found in temperate and tropical waters worldwide
■ Adult dolphins are on average 8ft to 12ft and weigh around 45⁄8kg. Males are bigger than females
■ Communicate through squeaks, whistles, snapping of jaws and leaping up to 20ft in the air
■ Acute sense of hearing, but poor sense of smell
■ Swim in groups of up to 12, known as pods. Can also form herds of up to 100 dolphins

GREAT WHITE SHARK
(Carcharodon carcharias)

■ Only its belly is white; it is grey to blue grey on top
■ Found along temperate coastlines around the world, including California, Australia, New Zealand
■ Adults are generally between 10ft and 15ft long. The record is 21ft. Females are bigger than males
■ Have 3,000 teeth at any one time. Do not chew their food, but rip off chunks and swallow them whole
■ Can swim through water at speeds of up to 43mph
■ About half to a third of known shark attacks each year are by great whites. Most are not fatal

---

THE DAY I WAS EATEN ALIVE

It's every swimmer's nightmare. In the week a surfer is butchered by a Great White, a British diver recalls his own terrifying shark attack

---

A great white shark: Common off the coast of South Australia

Bride's screams as her husband is eaten by shark

From **Richard Shears**
in Melbourne

A BRIDE on honeymoon watched in horror as her husband was torn to pieces by a great white shark.

Tina Bayes stayed on the beach while her husband Cameron, 26, paddled out to sea on his surfboard off the coast of South Australia.

As he turned round to wave at her the 12ft shark struck and dragged him under.

Other surfers said the shark initially appeared to release Mr Bayes, who somehow managed to get back on his board.

Seconds later, however, it grabbed him a second time and he was not seen again.

The shark then surfaced 500 yards from the beach, where it appeared to spit out a piece of surfboard.

With Mrs Bayes screaming from the shore, some of the other surfers paddled towards this area in search of her husband.

All they found was a pool of blood on the surface of the water.

The attack happened early yesterday off remote Cactus Beach, an area notorious for great whites.

Mr and Mrs Bayes, who were both New Zealanders, were on a working honeymoon in Australia.

Staying at campsites, Mr Bayes planned to earn money shearing sheep.

Surfer Jeff Hunter, who saw the attack, said: 'It was all very quick and very frightening.

'The shark had no hesitation. It took the surfer in a kind of circular motion.

'It looked horrendous,' Mr Hunter added. 'There was blood and surfboard everywhere.'

Mrs Bayes, who is also in her mid-twenties, was taken to hospital suffering from deep shock.

With no sign last night of her husband's body, a shark fisherman was called in to hunt down his killer over the next few days.

Great whites are common off Cactus Beach, which is reached from the famous highway which crosses the Nullabor Plain between Adelaide and Perth.

They feed off several seal colonies about two miles from shore and follow schools of salmon closer to shore.

Yesterday's attack was the first death of a surfer at the beach, although a local boy bled to death in 1975 after a great white shark bit off his leg while he was swimming.

Local surfboard maker Paul Gravelle said: 'Surfers are conscious of the risk of shark attack but we've always relied on the fact that there has never been a fatality here.'

Shark expert Rodney Fox, who needed more than 500 stitches after surviving an attack off the South Australian coast in 1963, said he would 'not feel comfortable' in the shark-infested waters of Cactus Beach.

'Unfortunately it's renowned as a great area to surf in,' he added.

'So you have this wonderful surfing area combined with one of the most dangerous stretches of water in the world.'

r.shears@dailymail.co.uk

Isn't that a killer shark under my surfboard?

By James Mills

A SURFER told yesterday how he came within inches of a deadly 6ft bull shark off the coast of Cornwall.

The terrifying encounter, the fifth sighting of a killer shark in as many weeks, suggests that it may only be a matter of time before a swimmer is attacked in British waters.

Luke Goodman, 30, said he was horrified when he realised it was a bull shark hovering beneath his board just 30 yards from the shore at Perran beach near Penzance.

He said: 'I swam straight under one and I knew what it was immediately. I was absolutely terrified because I know what these things are capable of.

'I immediately pulled my legs up.'

'More deadly than a great white'

Dispute claims that bull shark was sighted off Cornish coast

Tropical monster that will attack anything in its path

...nus leucas) is ...old subtropical ...be responsible ...s worldwide. ...perfectly and a ...a female can

grow to 11ft long and weigh 500lb. The males are smaller, at 7ft long and 200lb.

It hunts in shallow waters and has been known to attack people standing in knee-deep water. It detects prey though sonar and eats fish, turtles, birds, dolphins and other sharks. Car hub caps, a mannequin, an oboe and a human skull have all been found in the stomachs of bull sharks.

In the 1800s, Indians in Nicaragua gave it god-like status and offered human sacrifices stuffed with emeralds and gold.

yards off Port looke last month.
...later the same week, a 12ft make ...was seen a few miles by the coast in ...a popular resort of Bude.
...than later, holidaymakers rushed ...in the sea in panic at Crebbian ...ach, near Hayle, when another ...een within 30 yards of the shore. ...Holloway, of Newquay's ...Shark Aquarium, said: 'It was a ...shark. It's amazing. They have ...been reported north of Spain.' The fact that the shark had a

...round one is interesting. It would...
...it's be a basking shark and makos...
...and bull sharks have pointed noses.
'Bull sharks are fearless and one of the top shark species to tackle prey bigger fish themselves.

Experts say average sea temperatures of Britain have risen by more than 2 degrees this year, perhaps because of global warming, and this might be attracting tropical marine species to the South Coast.'

Luke.Goodman@mail.co.uk

Terrified: Luke Goodman

● PREDATORY: Bull sharks have a reputation for their aggression and for attacking their victims in shallow water

Shark sighting causes beach panic

■ **Continued from Page 1**

through the water column requires a high degree of experience and more so if you are engaged in another activity.'

Doug Herdson, from Plymouth's National Marine Aquarium, said: 'It is highly unlikely that this sighting was a bull shark. They have never been seen in European waters.'

Last month, youngsters were evacuated from Crebbian, near Hayle after a surfer thought he saw a make shark, the fastest swimming of the shark species, where a group of was long. Two weeks later, a group of was fishermen claimed they saw a mako leap out of the water a few miles off Bude, in North Cornwall.

Shark experts have cast some doubt on these sightings, saying they were most likely to be basking sharks, which are regularly seen and are harmless to people.

Yesterday, Mr Goodman, from Penzance, recalled the moment he believed he was just feet away from the shark.

'I was on a wave at the time and it swam straight underneath me, it must have been at least six feet long,' he said. 'I immediately pulled my legs up and surfed to the shore. I was

terrified I'd fall off but I made it to the beach.'

He ran along the beach shouting to other water-sports enthusiasts to get out of the water, setting off chaotic scenes as swimmers and surfers raced to the shore.

Bull sharks are off-white and grey and have a widespread distribution in the world's tropical and sub-tropical waters. It is considered the most dangerous shark, including people, anything in its path, because it attacks fish, and is found close to the shore hunting for prey in shallow waters.

The incident came as the RNLI chief lifeguard at Cornwall warned that there are 'thousands' of sharks off the county's coast, most of them harmless.

Steve Instance, who manages 200 lifeguards along 70 miles of coastline, said: ''It would be naive to think that there aren't sharks out there. There are makos and here are porbeagles as well as others, smaller than this. There are thousands of them, but in this country they don't trouble bathers.'

Although no sharks have been recorded off a British beach, the mako and the porbeagle shark have formidable reputations in other parts of the world, where attacks are frequent.

★★★★ Evening

Shark terror

Great white sighting off Devon beach sends surfers into panic

Deserted: normally crowded beach at Croyde was empty after the reported sighting

SURFERS were today staying away from a popular north Devon beach after the reported sighting of a great white shark.

The creature, described as being more than 12 feet long, was said to have been seen off Baggy Point, Croyde.

Great whites can grow up to 16 feet long, and have up to 3,000 teeth. They have never officially been recorded off a British beach.

But Chaynee Hodgetts, 15, who is on holiday with her parents, is adamant. She said: 'It was white on its belly and its back was grey.'

Chaynee, who hopes to pursue a career in

By Mark Prigg

She added: 'I realised it was not a basking shark and it was too long to be a porbeagle. I could get a very good idea of its size by comparing it with dolphins.'

Emily Hamilton works in a surf shop 500 yards from Baggy Point. She said: 'I think we are all very wary now and a lot of surfers here are refusing to go in the water until it cools down a bit, as they are

JAWS II

Could there be MORE than one maneater off the Cornish coast?

By Matthew Bayley

IT is fast, ferocious and likes to sneak up on its prey.

Which means the mako shark does not make the most relaxing of swimming companions.

So the news that two have been spotted off Cornwall in just two weeks could leave some bathers preferring to stay on the shore.

Yesterday beaches across the region were on red alert after a fisherman reported seeing a mako leaping from a popular tourist spot.

The 15ft predator – whose name is derived from Maori for 'maneater' – was spotted on Tuesday near Bude.

Alan Britton, 52, was terrified when he saw the shark – a cousin of the great white – leap from the water as he and three friends enjoyed a fishing trip.

"I couldn't believe it," he said.

Terrified: Alan Britton

every day that you have a predator like that just feet away.

"I am glad I didn't try to land it.

"It was the second mako shark to be spotted off the Cornish coast in just two weeks."

Last month...

called "mouthing" – basically testing whether you are edible.

"If a swimmer was there would..."

to 60mph...

Western Morning News SOUTH WEST DAILY

Gig rowers say blue shark swam under their boat 'looking for food'

● ON THE PROWL: The curator at Newquay's Blue Reef Aquarium says blue sharks do not attack people and are normally quite timid

Blue shark spotted in Cornish waters

Fiona Hann

A BLUE shark has been spotted swimming in waters off the West Cornwall coast...

NEWS

Thursday, August 18, 2005

The Mako shark: only a total of eight attacks have been reported worldwide.

'This is not Jaws visits Cornwall'

by IAN SHEPHERD

Western Morning News SOUTH WEST DAILY NEWSP

Shark warning as Mako spotted offsh

DAVID WILCOCK

SWIMMERS in seas around Westcountry beaches have been advised to leave the water if they spot sharks, after fishermen made the second sighting of a dangerous Mako shark this year.

● NO CATCH: Alan Britton, who spotted the Mako on a shark fishing trip, said he w

What to do if you meet creature in the water

lurk in our waters

FEARSOME PREDATOR:
A great white shark

Wildlife
SHARKS IN THE UK

Rare visitors

IT is unlikely that great whites travel to the UK on a regular basis in the same way that blue sharks do. If they did, we would certainly know about it.

But could the odd great white visit our shores by chance? After all, other big sharks turn up here. For instance, smooth hammerhead sharks migrate north from subtropical waters in summer and some stray into British waters.

Saturday, July 28, 2007   55p   thesun.co.uk

EXCLUSIVE: THE CORNISH JAWS

GREAT WHITE SHARK OFF UK

.CLUSIVE: GREAT

Just when you thought it was safe to go back to Cornwall

Poor publicity and taste for the exotic put sharks on danger list

Hannah Devlin

ARKS face a grave risk of ction because the ruling on European fishing is pring to weaken the ctions on finning, conser-sts say.

Shark Alliance, which in-leading oceanographers environmentalists, says third of the 130 species in are on the threatened l that another 20 per in immediate danger g them.

s' poor public image ll remember Jaws — o their under-protec-oja Fordham, the director of Shark aid. In British waters basking and spurdog ing with skates and the World Conser-n Red List.

ort published this Iliance says that the ce of shark fins, ing bigger by 5 per ear, has led to in-g of the animals practice of shark e dumping of a at sea after the fins.

Mayfair resta-shark fin soup d and a single a whale shark an fetch more Hong Kong he European emittee on a change in fishing.

hat 5 per cent meat caught

AT RISK OF EXTINCTION

SCOOPIN SHARK
Length: up to 6ft

ANGEL SHARK
Length: up to 6ft

WHALE SHARK
Length: up to 50ft

BASKING SHARK
Length: up to 50ft

Drawn to scale

DOGSHARK
(lifesize)

• Sharks have been on Earth for more than 400 million years, long before the time of the dinosaurs

• Sharks have the most powerful jaws on the planet. Unlike most animals' jaws, both the shark's upper and lower jaws move

• The smallest shark is the 8in dwarf dogshark and the largest is

the whale shark, which can grow to nearly 60ft

• There are about 400 species of sharks and more than 70 in European waters

• Sharks never run out of teeth. If one is lost, another moves forward from the rows of backup teeth

• Not all sharks are fierce carnivores – the enormous baskin and whale sharks both live on a diet of plankton

• Sharks are publicised "man-eaters" but people are more like to be killed by lightning than by shark

fishing boats to land fins and carcasses at separate ports.

eted, it will be a licence to fin and may well be actively coaxed

nerable to over-fishing as they grow slowly, mature late and

the accidental captu sharks by those fishin

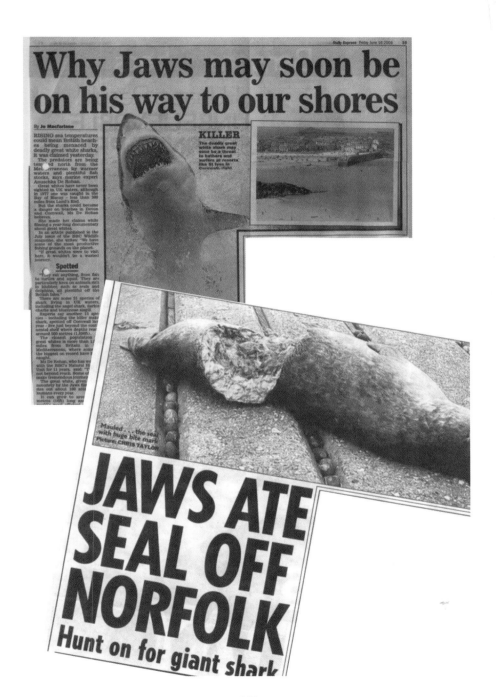

Why Jaws may soon be on his way to our shores

By Jo Macfarlane

RISING sea temperatures could mean British beaches being menaced by deadly great white sharks, it was claimed yesterday.

The predators are being tempted north from the Mediterranean by warmer waters and plentiful fish stocks, says marine expert Anouchka De Rohan.

Great whites have never been sighted in UK waters, although in 1977 one was caught in the Bay of Biscay – less than 300 miles from Land's End.

But the sharks could become a danger on beaches in Devon and Cornwall, Ms De Rohan believes.

She made her claims while filming a year-long documentary about great whites.

In an article published in the July issue of the BBC Wildlife magazine, she writes: "We have some of the most productive fishing grounds on the planet.

"If great whites were to visit here, it wouldn't be a wasted journey.

Spotted

"They eat anything, from fish to turtles and squid. They are particularly keen on animals rich in blubber such as seals and dolphins, all plentiful off the British Isles."

There are some 31 species of shark living in UK waters, including the angel shark, tarbot shark and bluntnose sixgill.

Experts say another 15 species – including the killer mako shark, spotted off Cornwall last year – live just beyond the continental shelf where depths reach around 500 metres (1,600ft).

The closest population of great whites is more than 1,000 miles from Britain in Mediterranean, where some of the biggest on record have been caught.

Ms De Rohan, who has worked with the BBC's Natural History Unit for 14 years, said: "I'm not beyond words. Some of them made tremendous journeys."

The great white, given notoriety by the Jaws films, rips out about 100 kilos of humans every year.

It can grow to around 6 metres (18ft) long and weigh

KILLER
The deadly great white shark may soon be a threat to bathers and surfers at resorts like St Ives in Cornwall, right

Mauled . . . the seal with huge bite marks
Picture: CHRIS TAYLOR

JAWS ATE SEAL OFF NORFOLK
Hunt on for giant shark

pits nature's greatest predator against caged ce

had their **bayest in Shark Alley**
sparked by ... ...
attack is the past year Cumbrian
businessman Mark Currie was
reported to have been attacked by
a Great White while cage-diving
there in December 2004.

Mr Currie's experience certainly
sounds terrifying. According to his
account, after making repeated
lunges at the cage, the 16ft creature
nearly chewed through the metal
bars, severed the connection to a
buoy nearly sending the cage to the
abyssl and generally traumatised
the hapless tourist.

He did, however, manage to film
the encounter and later sold the
photographs to a newspaper.

The truth, according to the Shark
Trust, is rather more prosaic. The
shark — which was considerably
smaller than 20ft — simply
'mouthed' the cage (a common
occurrence), did not try to bite
through the bars and at no time
was Mr Currie in any danger.

The damage done by this story
not only to shark eco-tourism but
to the image of sharks in general is
immense and irresponsible,' Ms
Hood says.

The case of Mr Currie is the latest
in a long line of myths surrounding
this most enigmatic of creatures.

The Ancient Greeks and Romans
were well aware that sharks could
attack and devour humans, and in
500BC historian Herodotus
described the most impressive
predator in the sea.

BUT IN relatively recent
times, a new myth took
hold: one that said that the
shark was harmless and
posed no threat to humans.

In 1891, Hermann Oelrichs, an
American socialite and millionaire,
bet $500 to anyone who could prove
that sharks attacked humans. To
make his point, he took a party of
observers out to sea, found a shoal
of large sharks, jumped in and
swam unharmed with the
predators for several minutes.

Then, in 1915, an article appeared
in the New York Times written by
the director of the American
Museum of Natural History, Dr
Fredrick Lucas. The article stated
the scientific consensus at the
time: sharks were timid creatures
whose bite was nowhere near
strong enough to damage a human.

All that changed in the summer of
1916. Along the Eastern seaboard of

the United States, sea-bathing had
become popular as the new rail-
ways allowed thousands of city
dwellers to escape the stifling heat.

But that year something very
large and nasty swam into the
inshore waters off the resorts,
sowing a panic and fear that has
still not abated whenever that
triangular fin is spotted in the sea.

Three men and a young boy lost
their lives when what is believed to

have been a Great White shark left
its usual deep water habitat and
headed for the beaches. The result
was predictable — and ghastly.

'His death was the most horrible
thing I ever saw,' said a witness to
the end of one Charles Vansant, who
had been swimming in just three-
and-a-half feet of water when something grabbed him from below.

The water boiled red with blood,
and Vansant popped back to the

surface, in a bad way. One of his legs
had been effectively filleted,
stripped of skin, muscle and
cartilage down to the bone. He died
from blood loss and shock.

After three more deaths and
several injuries, the rogue fish now
had a price on its head and after a
fierce struggle, it was finally killed
and found to have 15lb of human
flesh in its stomach.

The saga inspired Peter Benchley

associate humans with food

to write the novel Jaws, which was
later filmed by Steven Spielberg.

Sharks are certainly responsible
for some of the most horrible tales
of grisly death in history.

When the U.S. cruiser Indianapolis
was torpedoed in 1945 off the island
of Guam, more than 900 sailors
found themselves in the sea.

Over the next five days, a true-life
horror story played itself out. The
air was rent with the screams of
sailors eaten alive by a growing
pack of Tiger sharks. More than 400
were eaten.

Whatever their supporters say
(including Benchley himself, who
regrets having demonised the Great
White), sharks are dangerous.

YES, YOU are far more likely
to be killed on the drive to
the beach than swimming
in even the most shark-
infested waters.

And yes, if you are a Great White
you are millions of times more
likely to be killed by a human than
the other way round, thanks to
the toll taken by tuna fishermen's
long lines.

And it is important to realise that
sharks are not growing more
dangerous, or more common.

Overfishing is probably forcing
more sharks to come close to shore
in search of prey — increasing the
likelihood that they will come into
contact with swimmers, as the
popularity of watersports and
greatly increased tourism to
tropical waters sees more people in
the sea.

But all that said, there is something so uniquely horrible about the
thought of being eaten alive in an
alien environment that sharks will
probably never lose their terror in
the minds of most of us.

In an ever more sanitised world,
the possibility — however remote
— that we will become a meal for
an animal which evolved before the
dinosaurs provides an entertaining
frisson of fear whenever we
take a dip.

Surely we do not need caged
'celebrities' to make axe of the
most compelling animals ever to
have evolved even more exciting
than nature intended.

HAVE WE TURNED SHARKS INTO MAN EATERS?

The penny is slowly dropping and sharks are starting to get a fairer hearing and be portrayed accurately in some areas of the media.

Cartoon Chris Wylie.

Chapter Twelve

STRANGE AND TRUE

A random compendium of little known shark facts:

- British seas are home to at least 30 shark species.

- A Cornish fish merchant was slightly surprised when, having bought a Porbeagle Shark, he cut it open and found a whole pigeon inside. The pigeon's leg ring enabled its owner to be contacted, and he was amazed when he learnt where his pigeon had landed!

- The most northerly shark attack recorded occurred in British waters in 1960, when a young German sailor off northern Scotland was bitten by a small shark caught in a net.

- A mermaid's purse is an egg case that may well have contained a baby shark.

- The 'rock salmon' that used to be commonly on sale in British fish and chip shops was actually shark – Spiny Dogfish.

- Many of Dublin's street lamps were once fuelled by oil from Basking Sharks' livers.

- In 1961 the Shark Angling Club recorded 6000 Blue Sharks caught off Looe in Cornwall by boats reporting to the club. In 2000 the figure had dropped to 86.

- In December 2006 the Angelshark was declared "locally extinct" in the North Sea by ICES (International Council for the Exploration of the Seas)

- Blue Sharks caught and tagged off Cornwall have more than once been re-caught off the eastern United States.

- In Britain there has only ever been one real recorded shark "attack". Cows are statistically more dangerous to Britons than sharks!

- There is much speculation about how the Porbeagle Shark got its name, and there are many theories. One is that it comes from the Cornish "porth" for harbour and "bugel" meaning shepherd.

- Many sharks "breach" or leap out of the water, including the Great White, Mako, Thresher and Basking Shark. But few people will ever get as close to a shark breaching as Ross Staplehurst and Danny Vokins, when a 181 kilo, 4.5 metre unhooked, free-swimming Thresher Shark jumped into their 6.7 metre (22 foot) boat off the Isle of Wight in June 1981

- At Mr Kai's restaurant in London's Mayfair in 2006, bowls of sharks fin soup were on the menu at a cost of £108 each

- In 1977, a Japanese trawler pulled up the decayed remains of a Basking Shark, which was mistaken for a sea monster (a plesiosaur). Basking Sharks are known to decompose into "pseudoplesiosaur" forms and their carcasses have often been mistaken for sea monsters.

- Tagging has established that Soupfin Sharks (Tope) can live for more than 50 years.

- Basking Sharks may well filter more than 1800 cubic metres of water an hour. That is roughly the equivalent of an Olympic swimming pool.

- In 1986 a research team went to the Canary Islands to find out what had been biting fibre optic cables between Tenerife and Gran Canaria. The culprit turned out to be none other than the Kitefin Shark, a species also found in British waters.

- From "Shark Attack" by H. David Baldridge. "In reply to a question concerning the Royal Navy's wartime need for an effective shark repellent, Prime Minister Winston Churchill assured the House of Commons that "...the British Government is entirely opposed to sharks".

- The Greenland Shark is the only shark to live in the Arctic Sea and reputedly lures prey fish by using white, possibly luminous, parasitic copepods attached to its eyes.

- In August 1956 off Cornwall the Royal Navy decided to blow up what they thought was a dangerous shark. The shark had other ideas and blew up the Royal Navy. (See page 90)

- In April 1995 the People reported that a mother and her three children were treated by ambulancemen having inhaled fumes from a dead shark. It had been kept in formaldehyde and other toxic preservatives and left at their home.

- Male Blue Sharks are very aggressive during mating and grip the females with their teeth during the process. However, female Blue Sharks have skin two-to-three times the thickness of males to give them some protection during these amorous encounters.

- Legend has it that Blue Sharks will follow a ship on which someone has died waiting for the body to be committed to the sea.

- In 1989 fifty-seven Basking Sharks swam into Peel harbour on the Isle of Man. It was one of three large schools that came close inshore on the west side of the island that year.

- The Cookiecutter * or Cigar Shark swallows its teeth. It is thought it does this to extract the calcium.

- Sharks have swum in our oceans for more than 400 million years, predating even dinosaurs.

- Sharks never run out of teeth. Depending on species they may grow over 20,000 in their lifetime and when one falls out another moves into position to take its place.

- They have the strongest jaws of any animals on the planet.

- Shark skeletons are made out of cartilage, which is lighter and more flexible than bone.

- Unlike other fish their skin is not made up of scales but of thousands of tiny toothlike denticles. Their skin is highly abrasive and has been used in place of sandpaper.

- Sharks, as a group, include an amazing diversity of species. They range in size from less than 30 centimetres to over 20 metres, and are found in the shallowest and deepest water.

- The fastest swimming shark is thought to be the Shortfin Mako which has been clocked achieving speeds of 69 kilometres an hour for short bursts.

- Sandtiger * Shark pups are cannibals before they are born. Pups not only eat infertile eggs while still in the uterus but also eat other developing pups.

- Tiger * Sharks give a new meaning to being omnivorous. Car licence plates, a chair leg, human body parts, birds and turtles are among the many items found in their stomachs.

- On November 2nd 2011 Tom Huxley and his girlfriend were walking home in Aberystwyth when they smelt something decidedly fishy in the air. They investigated and found a very dead Blue Shark parked in the side of the road on a double yellow line. Aberystwyth was having major problems since its two traffic wardens stopped working six months earlier prior to their functions being restarted under police control. The shark which had obviously been dumped was gone a couple of hours later, having presumably been removed by the council or the police.

* THESE SHARKS ARE NOT FOUND IN BRITISH SEAS.

Chapter Thirteen

THE FIN EDGE OF LUNACY
Bycatch, discards, CITES

It has always seemed depressingly illogical to me that humans have managed to put men into space, create artificial hearts and invent weapons capable of destroying the world, yet we don't seem to be able to solve the problem of bycatch, and the wasteful discarding at sea of fish which legislation says can't be landed even when caught accidentally.

In 2011 Channel 4 screened a series of programmes about the sea presented by celebrity chefs. Gordon Ramsay's show 'Shark Bait' probably had the largest audience, and attracted the most attention, but once the hullaballoo had died down it had achieved little apart from raising public awareness. In contrast Hugh Fearnley-Whittingstall's 'Fish Fight' programmes concentrated on bycatch issues and achieved positive results.

His statement that "half of all the fish caught in the North Sea are thrown back overboard DEAD", struck a real chord with the public and at the time of writing over three quarters of a million people have signed up to his 'Fish Fight Campaign', adding their names to the following letter which will be sent to Commissioner Maria Damanaki and all the members of the European Parliament.

The letter reads as follows:-

"I have seen the images of dead and dying fish discarded in European waters. I understand that the current Common Fisheries Policy leads to discarding on a vast scale for example half of all fish caught in the North Sea are being discarded because of the current quota system imposed by the CFP.

I want this senseless waste of food to end. I want you to use your influence to stop this unacceptable and shameful practice. I am supporting the 'Fish Fight' campaign to help bring about this vital change in our seas".

The bycatch issue affects many shark species, with the Porbeagle and the Spurdog being of particular current concern. I have already mentioned large Porbeagle catches which occurred due to their having aggregated. Forming aggregations doesn't only make a species vulnerable to targeted fisheries but to bycatch as well, and in August 2011 a large Porbeagle bycatch was reported near Lundy Island. Three commercial vessels were involved in catching over 200 Porbeagle sharks to the southwest of the island. Only one shark was alive which was released. I must stress that commercial vessels involved in bycatch are breaking no laws. The fishing industry regards bycatch as a major problem, discarding as a wasteful practice, and are working with the science and conservation sectors to address this.

The following is an extract from the November 2011 issue of Shark Focus, the Shark Trust magazine. The article discusses bycatch and discard issues.

"DISCARDS: WOULD A TOTAL BAN WORK?

Definitions
Discards are the portion of a catch of fish which are not retained on board during commercial fishing operations and are returned, often dead or dying, to the sea.

Bycatch: The term **"bycatch"** is usually used for fish caught unintentionally in a fishery while targetting other fish or an unwanted portion of a mixed fishery. Bycatch may comprise different species, undersized individuals of the target species, or juveniles of the target species.

A total discards ban is certainly a neat request: a simple and unambiguous message and, for some species, could be an appropriate element of more sustainable fisheries management. But is it that simple, and why are many shark conservationists concerned that a total discards ban could lead to greater impacts on shark, skate and ray populations?

This article will briefly explore some of the issues which complicate and challenge the applicability of a total discards ban for elasmobranchs (sharks, skates and rays). This piece is intended as an observation and does not represent a formal position statement from the Shark Trust.

Survival: In comparison to bony fish, sharks have a robust physiology – their cartilaginous skeleton gives them greater flexibility, the absence of a swim bladder leaves them less affected by changes in pressure, and dermal denticles provide a tough outer skin, which are all features that improve their chance of discard survival.

However, discard survival is dependent on a number of factors – gear type, time the nets/lines are in the water (soak time), the weight of the catch, the time on deck and handling all influence the likely chance of survival.

Historically discarded: Historically sharks, perhaps with the exception of Spurdog and some skate, were discarded. And with a conservative life history strategy (slow growth, late maturity and few young) this discarding ensured that as many sharks as possible had the opportunity to contribute to population growth.

With the decline in other traditional target stocks fisheries diversified, and in the early 90's there was an increase in the retention rate of previously discarded sharks. This increased retention, linked with non-effective/existent catch limits saw the populations of some species decline dramatically. To put it simply, the practice of retaining previously discarded species further impacted upon shark populations.

Current management implications: Sharks are caught as bycatch and in mixed fisheries. Under current fisheries management regimes the need for precautionary management of Endangered or Critically Endangered species such as Porbeagle or Spurdog has resulted in a scenario of a zero Total Allowable Catch (TAC) and a prohibition on the retention of bycatch. The stringent nature of this level of management reflects the concern over populations which have exhibited population declines of more than 80%.

However a zero TAC does not equate to zero catch (just zero landings), and these species may be inadvertently caught in quite substantial numbers, leading to a scenario of discarding often dead animals which infuriates fishers and concerns conservationists.

The images of fishers discarding dead or dying fish is a powerful one; add to this the situation where current fisheries management for elasmobranchs often prevents the retention of bycatch, and we are faced with a challenging scenario.

Solution? So, if despite stringent management, sharks are still bycaught and discarding of both dead and live animals still occurs, what is the solution – in fact is there one?

In the context of unwanted bycatch or species under precautionary management, the Shark Trust remains adamant that any shark which might survive should be given opportunity to do so, and returned to the water with due haste and care. Under current management regimes, to ensure this occurs the Trust has no choice but to support the ban on retention of bycatch for zero TAC species. However, the matter of dead discarding associated with bycatch prohibitions and other fisheries is of great concern, as the current requirement to discard all animals (dead or alive) does nothing to reduce mortality and therefore improve the conservation status of the species.

So here's where we need to go back to first principles – when a species is vulnerable and in need of stringent protection we need to work with the fishers to avoid catching the species in the first place. Unfortunately the inevitable truth will be that sharks will continue to be caught, and so we must work closely with the fishing industry to develop practical measures to ensure the highest chance of avoidance or survival if caught, whilst recognising the nonsensical nature of dead discarding.

So is a total discards ban the way forwards? For bony fish it makes sense, but as ever the situation is just not that simple.

The European Commission proposes to eliminate the practice of throwing unwanted fish overboard by 2016, recognising that such discards are an unacceptable waste of resources. However, the Commission does state that species with a high expected survival rate should not be covered by the landing obligation – that they should be released. This is a position the Shark Trust wholly supports. **//**

The salient point for sharks is that landing means no chance of survival at all, which is why the Trust's article ends by advocating that bycatch avoidance and survival if caught are the key aspects which need our attention.

Of the sharks that were bycatch near Lundy in August 2011 one was definitely known to be alive, but there may well have been others. On an expedition in Qatar in 2009 I was called to look at a pile of dead Whitecheek sharks which were lying in a heap on the quay in the sun. I worked out that they had been out of the water for at least 45 minutes, but probably over an hour. I sifted through them and saw the gills moving in one of the little sharks. I picked it up, took it back to the water, swum it forward and off it went. There were 15 sharks and the outcome was that seven were revived and swum off strongly, two couldn't be revived and were despatched, and six were dead and beyond hope. In this case the survival rate was just under 50%.

My friend Ken Watterson who was a leading Basking Shark researcher on the Isle of Man in the 1980's remembers a shark which had been lying on the quay at Peel Harbour, and which Ken believes had been out of the water for over two hours. He observed a muscle twitching next to the shark's eye, and began to wonder just how dead the shark was. They rolled the animal off the quay and back into the water and swum it forward. This dead shark revived and swum off, whether it survived in the long term we don't know but at least it had a chance.

I have not been able to find any relevant research on survival rates of elasmobranchs once they have been out of the water and dry for a period, and/or appear to be dead. However the two instances that I have recounted indicate that survival among sharks returned as bycatch might be higher than is widely recognised.

– – – – – –

I started this chapter by stating that it seemed illogical that we could put men into space but couldn't solve the problem of bycatch and discard. I believe this issue will be solved, or at least measures will be introduced which will improve the situation as it is today. Hugh Fearnley-Whittingstall aimed to get 250,000 signatures for his 'Fish Fight' campaign by the end of summer 2011; he got three times this number and has helped firmly position this issue on the political agenda. The European Commission proposes to eliminate the practice of discarding by 2016, and the UK Minister Richard Benyon MP has publicly voiced his commitment to reduce bycatch and address discards, acknowledging the requirements of sharks and other long living species.

The fishing industry is committed to finding working solutions, as are marine conservationists, so if when I next revise this book I can't report meaningful progress I will be very disappointed.

– – – – – –

CITES – The shark conservation community worldwide had high hopes of the 15th CITES meeting that was held in Doha, Qatar in April 2010. The following species were all proposed for Appendix II listing which prohibits trade in the species by CITES listed nations.

Scalloped, Great and Smooth Hammerheads, Sandbar Sharks, Dusky Sharks, Oceanic Whitetips, Porbeagles, and Spurdogs.

None of these sharks actually got Appendix II listing, and headlines around the world attested to the disappointment of many – CITES SELL OUT, CITES TOOTHLESS TIGER, SHARKS SOLD OUT IN DOHA.

None of the species proposed were borderline cases. Each of the 8 species for which a listing was sought had a compelling science and fact based case so why was nothing achieved?

I heard rumours that tactical voting, and commercial interests had influenced the outcome. I hope that the passage of three years leading up to the next CITES meeting in Thailand will allow stronger cases to be better prepared, and that those nations who were in opposition at the Doha meeting will have been won round.

I have several friends working in various departments in the government of Qatar, and have led three Shark Conservation Society expeditions to that country. At the end of the CITES meeting I got a call from a Qatari friend in Doha "Richard, your expeditions have done more for sharks in the Gulf than CITES!". It was a joke and meant light-heartedly, but sadly it was true.

Chapter Fourteen

SHARK FISHERIES, THE CONSERVATION AND FUTURE OF OUR SHARKS (IUCN RED LIST), AND A RAY OF HOPE FROM CHINA

Few creatures on land or sea have been as unsustainably and often cruelly exploited as sharks. All the large species found in our waters are seriously depleted and many of our smaller sharks are also listed as threatened or critically endangered.

Research carried out by the Dalhousie University in Nova Scotia, Canada, has produced figures based on 15 years of catch reports from the western Atlantic. Regrettably, there is no similar research for the eastern side of the Atlantic. However, it is reasonable to assume that for some species the position is similar and, for others, virtually the same. The Blue Shark, for example, is involved in a continual circular migration around the north Atlantic and is one population, and so the western Atlantic figures will probably to an extent apply to the eastern side.

Fishing pressures on many shark species have not slackened appreciably since the research was published so the depletion rates today may well be even higher. The Dalhousie figures relevant to some species found in British waters were as follows:

Blue Shark - depleted by 60 per cent
Shortfin Mako - increasing decline
Thresher Shark - depleted by 80 per cent
Hammerhead Shark - depleted by 89 per cent

The high value of fins has meant that sharks have ceased to be nuisance by-catch, which, if put back, would have a chance of survival. Instead, they have become a highly valuable targeted catch, or wanted bycatch. Longline fishing boats traditionally targeted tuna, swordfish, marlin, and others. Lines of more than 20 kilometres are usual with baited hooks every two to three metres. The deployment of just one line can catch hundreds of sharks. To ease storage and transportation problems and avoid taking the time required to kill the shark (as well as not having the risk of shark flesh tainting other fish), the sharks are often finned and thrown back into the ocean while still alive, to die a slow and painful death.

Different species are caught for different reasons, but the single most important reason that most large sharks are caught is for their fins. As the economies of China and other Far Eastern nations have developed, shark fin soup has become an affordable luxury for an ever-increasing market. Shamefully, the European Union is one of the leading suppliers of fins to those markets. Spanish fishing fleets harvest enormous numbers of sharks and supplied about 11 per cent of the total Hong Kong fin market in 2005.

By 2011 most E.U. countries were working on the basis of sharks having to be landed with 'fins naturally attached' (FNA). However the Spanish and Portuguese governments were still using Special Fishing Permits which allowed the landing of fins without bodies. It is hoped that this position will have changed by the end of 2012 when the review of the E.U. Shark Finning Regulation is ratified on an E.U. wide basis. The E.U. remains a significant supplier of fins to the world market, and so all actions taken to better manage shark fisheries must be welcomed.

The Porbeagle Shark is very vulnerable to over fishing due to its tendency to aggregate (form groups), which makes it easy prey for longliners. Cases of large Porbeagle catches by longliners in the UK were in 2003, when one longliner was reported to have taken more than 130 sharks off south Cornwall, and in August 2007, when another took between 60 and 90 sharks near Lundy Island in the Bristol Channel. These were two incidences that I became aware of, but it is safe to say that there will have been other such catches I didn't hear about, and gill-netting is another fishing method that results in large scale shark catches. In 2009 the E.U. imposed a zero TAC (Total Allowable Catch) on Porbeagles which currently puts an end to the commercial targeting of this species. However anglers can still target

Porbeagles and commercial bycatch remains a huge problem. In 2011 over 200 Porbeagles were caught in nets near Lundy and due to a ban on being able to land them they had to be dumped at sea. The fishermen cannot be blamed for accidental bycatches, and developing rules to deal with bycatch and discards remains a challenge for policy makers and conservationists. In November 2011 the E.U. extended measures to protect Porbeagles by recognising that the previous levels of protection had not applied to all European waters, and notably not to the Mediterranean. The new extended protection included the Mediterranean, and of course applied to E.U. vessels internationally wherever they fished. One estimate I read suggested that the Porbeagle population in the Mediterranean had declined by 99% since the mid twentieth century. The small loophole allowing anglers to target and catch Porbeagles would effectively be closed if the anglers were required by law to return the sharks to the sea. This issue is currently being worked upon and it is expected measures will be put into law by the Scottish government early in 2012. It is hoped that England and Wales would then follow.

In 2005, a Lowestoft-based company was planning a specific trade in Soupfin Sharks. Like Porbeagles, Soupfin Sharks (Tope) have a tendency to school that makes them vulnerable to over fishing. However, the venture was shelved, partly due to the efforts of various activist groups, and partly for economic reasons.
All of the species mentioned in this book as British sharks appear on the IUCN Red List of Threatened Species. (See the following table):

IUCN Red List Status of British Sharks Species
(Source – International Union for the Conservation of Nature, Shark Specialist Group).

Species	NEA (Catagory)	Global (Catagory)	Year
Angelshark		Critically Endangered	2006
Spiny Dogfish (Spurdog)	Critically Endangered	Vulnerable	2006
Porbeagle Shark	Critically Endangered	Vulnerable	2005
Portuguese Dogfish	Endangered	Vulnerable	2008*
Leafscale Gulper Shark	Endangered	Vulnerable	2008*
Basking Shark	Endangered	Vulnerable	2000
Thresher Shark		Vulnerable	2008*
Shortfin Mako		Vulnerable	2008*
Angular Roughshark		Vulnerable	2007
Soupfin Shark (Tope)		Vulnerable	2005
Nursehound		Near Threatened	2008*
Sharpnose Sevengill Shark		Near Threatened	2007
Bluntnose Sixgill Shark		Near Threatened	2003

Porbeagles in crates in Newlyn market awaiting sale. © Jed Trewin

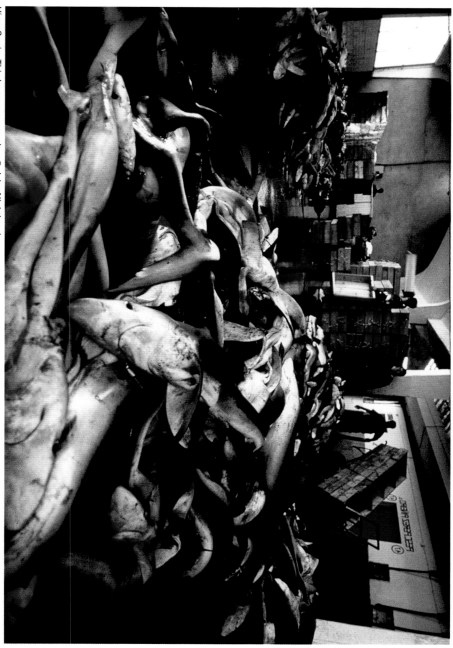

Vigo, Spain. This happens everyday. © John Nightingale

Species	NEA (Catagory)	Global (Catagory)	Year
Frilled Shark		Near Threatened	2003
Blue Shark		Near Threatened	2000
Smooth Hammerhead		Near Threatened	2000
Black Dogfish	Near Threatened	Least Concern	2008*
Velvet Belly	Near Threatened	Least Concern	2005
Greenland Shark	Near Threatened	Least Concern	2005
Blackmouth Catshark		Least Concern	2008*
Smallspotted Catshark		Least Concern	2008*
Ghost Catshark		Least Concern	2004
Birdbeak Dogfish		Least Concern	2003
Longnose Velvet Dogfish		Least Concern	2003
Starry Smoothound		Least Concern	2000
Smoothound		Least Concern	2000
Great Lanternshark		Data Deficient	2008*
Knifetooth Dogfish		Data Deficient	2008*
Sailfin Roughshark		Data Deficient	2008*
Iceland Shark		Data Deficient	2007
Velvet Dogfish		Data Deficient	2005
Whiteghost Catshark		Data Deficient	2004
Bramble Shark		Data Deficient	2003
Kitefin Shark		Data Deficient	2000

(*Data "in preparation" at the time of going to press).
(NEA = North East Atlantic)

In total, 30 per cent of British sharks are considered threatened. Of these, 9 per cent (three species) are "Critically Endangered", 9 per cent (three species) are "Endangered" and 12 per cent (four species) are "Vulnerable". A further 26 per cent (nine species) are considered "Near Threatened". Only seven species (21 per cent) are considered to be of Least Concern, and, currently, too little is known about eight species (23 per cent) to be able to assess them beyond "Data Deficient". These species will be re-assessed as soon as more information becomes available.

While many of the deepwater sharks on the list are categorised "Data deficient", scientists know enough about their life histories to recognise the urgent need for their protection. Deepwater sharks such as the Portuguese Dogfish and the Leafscale Gulper Shark were targeted by a gill net fishery off north west Scotland, and had their populations reduced by over 80 per cent. Their liver oil (squalene) and meat (siki) are valuable products that made the trade worthwhile. The fishery is now closed to gill nets, but is still open to deepwater trawls and longlining, and the damage to shark populations will take decades to repair. It is thought likely that the Leafscale Gulper Shark has a particularly long two-year gestation period and produces only five to eight pups per pregnancy, so perhaps decades is optimistic! With such a low reproductive capability recovery may actually take hundreds of years.

As mentioned previously in Chapter 6 sustained over fishing of Angelsharks and Spurdogs (Spiny Dogfish) has pushed both populations to the edge of collapse in British waters. Indeed the Angelshark was declared extinct in the North Sea in 2006. The Basking Shark now enjoys protection but was once taken in enormous numbers (see Chapter 4). This species was actively hunted until the 1990's, and despite being protected in European waters, two Basking Sharks were landed in Belgium in 2007 and ended up being offered for sale in Bruges market. In March 2008 the Angelshark received long awaited protection in English and Welsh waters out to six nautical miles under the Wildlife and Countryside Act (1981), then in 2011 this was extended to twelve miles. The Angelshark is also a prohibited species under the E.U. Common Fisheries Policy, and is protected from recreational activity in England, Wales and Northern Ireland. However the same level of protection in Scottish waters has yet to be achieved.

The zero TAC limit first announced for Porbeagles and Spurdogs in 2009 allowed the landing of limited bycatch. These provisions had ceased by 2010, and together with the measures announced in November 2011, meant that both these species now have effective European protection from commercial landings, but not from bycatch. TAC's are subject to annual review as are bycatch provisions.

Some species including the Thresher already have a degree of protection under ICCAT (International Commission for the Conservation of Atlantic Tuna), and the Shortfin Mako and Blue Shark are now starting to get the attention they so badly need. With the effective cessation of commercial targeting of Spurdogs and Soupfin Sharks the evidence is that Smoothhounds (Starry) are becoming the next target for commercial fishing activity.

I have often heard it said that the only good shark is a dead shark, and have been asked why we need sharks. Wouldn't we be better off if this "dangerous-to-man" predator disappeared altogether?

My answers are as follows:
- The moral argument. In Britain we pride ourselves on fairness. The annual killing by hunting of up to 19,000 foxes provoked a fierce debate that rumbled on for years. Yet the fact that between 26 and 73 million sharks

have been taken annually by unsustainable fisheries and pushed towards extinction has started to be a concern only recently. It cannot be morally right that one of earth's newest arrivals (mankind) should be systematically wiping out a whole group of species that are among the oldest inhabitants of our planet.

- Self interest. Life on earth as we know it needs healthy oceans to survive. Oceans stay healthy only if marine eco-systems remain in balance. Science has shown that the removal of the apex predator from ocean food chains causes modification and, sometimes, the collapse of marine eco-systems. Self- interest should dictate that man recognises that sick seas could herald an uninhabitable planet. Sharks and other apex marine predators are a major part of this equation.

- The emotional argument. To me, sharks are one of the most beautiful animals on earth. They are also relatively harmless compared with many other sea and land creatures that are responsible for far more human deaths. How can we destroy these beautiful creatures largely for the sake of boring, bland-tasting bowls of soup? The television presenter Monty Halls likens the wiping out of sharks to the wholesale slaughter of the North American plains bison. Plains, which were home to teeming herds of millions of buffalo, are now empty. In parts of the North Atlantic the ocean is now missing between 80 to 90 per cent of those sharks that were there 50 years ago.

- Economic benefit. In several countries sharks are producing large revenues for eco-tourist operators and, thereby, supporting local businesses. A dead shark is "one time usage", whereas shark catch-and-release, and shark watching are repeat multi-usages, which generate a great deal more money. My view is that the only way wildlife will survive co-existing with man is by paying its way. Sharks can be long-term earners, and this alone is a powerful argument for their future.

Sharks mature late, have long gestation periods and then produce only a few young. British and European legislators are starting to act effectively and there are hopeful signs. In the three years since the first edition of this book the following legal steps have been taken to protect our sharks.

2009 Closure of Porbeagle target fishery in EU waters; zero TAC implemented / EU adopts Community Plan of Action for Sharks / UK Marine and Coastal Access Act passed / Angelshark, Common Skate, White Skate, Black Skate and Undulate Ray designated 'Prohibited Species' for all vessels in EU waters / Zero TAC implemented for deepwater sharks in EU waters / Global Shark Alliance is formed.

2010 Zero TAC implemented for Spiny Dogfish in EU waters (with bycatch allowance) / EU Common Fisheries Policy under review / Cessation of Special

Fishing Permits for UK commercial fishing fleet – all sharks landed by UK vessels anywhere in the world must have fins naturally attached / EU Shark Finning Regulation 1185/2003 under review / Porbeagles designated 'Prohibited Species' for all EU vessels in international waters / Development of network of Marine Conservation Zones(MCZ) continues: MCZ's to be operational by 2012.

2011 DEFRA release UK Shark, Skate and Ray Conservation Plan / EU shark finning regulation 1185/2003 review goes to public consultation / Zero TAC upheld for Spiny Dogfish in EU waters (no bycatch allowance) / Guitarfishes designated 'Prohibited Species' for all vessels in EU waters

These steps should prevent the aforementioned species from joining the Angelshark on the local extinction list.

The bad image sharks have due to their occasional attacks on man doesn't help them gain human supporters, nor does their being classified as fish. Fish are part of our diet and come under fisheries management policies. Wildlife is regarded differently, and were sharks deemed to be wildlife rather than fish, they would probably get considerably more effective protection. As it happens, the life cycles of some sharks are closer to those of mammals than fish.

––––––

On more than one occasion in these pages I have referred to the demand for shark fins as being the main reason for the unsustainable overfishing of sharks. China consumes 95% of the world's supply of shark fins and the laws of supply and demand mean that if the demand were able to be stopped there would be no reason for the supply.

In March 2011 I became aware of moves in China being made to try and bring in legislation that would ban the import of shark fins. Jim Zhang, a Chinese conservationist and two Chinese politicians had put proposals through the Peoples National Congress and the Chinese People's Political Consultative Congress to bring such a ban into law. My initial reaction was scepticism and incredulity, but investigation showed that both reactions were wrong. Moves were indeed afoot, they were serious, and had a chance of success.

Such potentially game changing initiatives needed recognising and encouraging, and the Shark Trust decided to present Shark Champion awards to the three Chinese potential shark saviours. I flew to Beijing to present the awards in June and discovered that WildAid were also working hard towards a ban. My initial scepticism and incredulity was replaced by the conviction that a ban would indeed come into law. The question is how long will the process take, and will a future import ban come in time to save the world's sharks? If I wasn't an optimist I wouldn't do what I do, so I have to believe the activists in China will get their law passed which will cut 95% of the world's demand for shark fins. With virtually no demand the supply will decrease and disappear.

In the meantime however those of us working outside China must keep trying to limit the supply and bring about sustainable shark fisheries. In the 18 years I have been working on shark conservation I have observed an enormous rise in public awareness of the plight faced by sharks, and increasingly around the world laws are being passed giving protection to many species.

－－－－－－

The Shark Trust in the UK spearheads campaigns aimed at raising public awareness of the vulnerability of sharks. It is also involved in lobbying EU and UK government agencies to ensure effective action against shark finning, sustainable fisheries policies, and other shark management measures. In addition to the Shark Trust, the World Wildlife Fund, the Marine Conservation Society, the International Fund for Animal Welfare, the Shark Alliance, Bite Back, The Shark Conservation Society, Greenpeace, Sea Shepherd, the Wildlife Trusts, IUCN (SSG), various angling groups, and statutory agencies are all active in a variety of shark conservation strategies.

So, now, an unashamed plug! At the time of writing, I am Chairman of the Shark Trust and if, in this book, I have managed to interest you in sharks, and to make you worry about their future then please visit the Trust's website www.sharktrust.org and consider becoming a registered supporter.

Becoming a Shark Trust supporter is one way you can help ensure these beautiful and wonderful creatures continue to exist for future generations on a healthy planet. It is appropriate therefore that this chapter should end with a comment from Ali Hood the Trust's Director of Conservation.

"In recent years many positive steps have been taken towards securing a more sustainable future for Britain's shark species; however there remains much to be done. Working closely with industry and governments we need to address the issues of bycatch and discards. We must recognise the shark species that currently have no management such as Shortfin Makos, Blue Sharks, Smoothhounds and Catsharks, and secure effective catch limits before recovery plans become a necessity. At the same time we must try to ensure that the UK government continues to champion shark conservation measures at home and on the high seas."

Reference Section

THE SHARK DIRECTORY

RESIDENT/REGULAR VISITORS

Angelshark
Basking Shark
Blue Shark
Greenland Shark
Nursehound Shark
Porbeagle Shark
Bluntnose Sixgill Shark
Sharpnose Sevengill Shark
Shortfin Mako Shark
Smallspotted Catshark
Smoothhound Shark
Starry Smoothhound Shark
Soupfin Shark (Tope)
Spurdog Shark (Spiny Dogfish)
Thresher Shark

RARE/DEEPWATER

Angular Roughshark
Sailfin Roughshark

Birdbeak Dogfish
Leafscale Gulper Shark

Black Dogfish
Great Lantern Shark
Velvet Belly Shark

Bramble Shark

Blackmouth Catshark

Frilled Shark

Ghost Catshark
Iceland Catshark
Whiteghost Catshark

Kitefin Shark

Longnose Velvet Dogfish
Knifetooth Dogfish
Velvet Dogfish

Portuguese Dogfish

Smooth Hammerhead

CLASSIFICATION OF SHARKS

Sharks are divided into eight major groups or orders.

Hexanchiformes — Six or seven gill slits, one dorsal fin.
Squaliformes — Five gill slits, two dorsal fins, short snout.
Pristiophoriformes — Five or six gill slits, two dorsal fins, snout long and saw-like.
Squatiniformes — Five gill slits, two dorsal fins, long and saw-like snout, flattened body.
Heterodontiformes — Five gill slits, two dorsal fins, dorsal fin spines.
Orectolobiformes — Five gill slits, two dorsal fins, mouth well in front of eyes.
Lamniformes — Five gill slits, two dorsal fins, no nictating eyelid.
Carcharhiniformes — Nictating eyelid, five gill slits, two dorsal fins.

REPRODUCTION

More than 450 different sharks in eight orders reproduce in different ways.

- Oviparity. This describes egg laying. These hatch externally and about forty per cent of sharks are born this way. After fertilisation, each egg is enclosed in a tough, flexible case known to many as a mermaid's purse. This method applies to Catsharks, Epaulette Sharks, Horn sharks and others.
- Ovoviviparity. This involves the females retaining the eggs. They then absorb the yolk, the young animal develops and hatches inside the mother and is born fully developed. About 25 per cent of sharks reproduce this way including Whale Shark, and the Spurdog (Spiny Dogfish) which is a resident in British seas.
- Oophagy. Some members of the lamnid family produce large numbers of infertile eggs and only one fertile egg in each ovary. The infertile eggs are eaten by the young in utero. Sandtiger Sharks (not a British species) go one stage further with pups in the uterus not only eating infertile eggs but also each other.
- Placental viviparity. This method is closest to that of most mammals and involves a placenta and an umbilical cord providing a link between the mother and the embryo. This is the most advanced method of reproduction found in sharks and applies to around 10 per cent of species.

RESIDENTS AND REGULAR VISITORS

ANGELSHARK
(Squatina squatina)

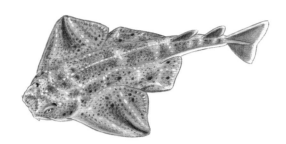

Size: Maximum 2.4 metres (7ft 8 ins)
Identification: Large and squat. Reddish-grey brown back with dots and spots.
Distribution: N.E. Atlantic, Mediterranean, Black Sea.
Habitat: Inshore down to 150 metres. Mostly on the bottom.
Diet/Behaviour: Skates, flatfish, molluscs, crustaceans. Rests by day,
                    hunts by night.
Biology: Ovoviviparous. Up to 25 pups a litter.
Status (IUCN)   Critically endangered

BASKING SHARK
(Cetorhinus maximus)

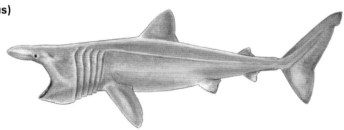

Size: Maximum 10 metres (32/33 ft)
Identification: Grey to bronzy brown, often mottled. Lighter below.
Distribution: Worldwide in temperate seas.
Habitat: Coast to continental shelf edge.
Diet/Behaviour: Plankton feeder. Highly migratory. Often seen breaching.
Biology: Probably oophagy. A litter of 6 pups reported.
Status (IUCN)   Vulnerable

BLUE SHARK
(Prionace glauca)

Size:	Maximum 3.8 metres (12 ft 5 ins)
Identification:	Blue back, lighter blue sides, white below. Slim shark, long snout.
Distribution:	Worldwide in temperate and tropical waters.
Habitat:	Migratory, pelagic & oceanic. Rarely found close inshore.
Diet/Behaviour:	Squid, pelagic fish, small sharks, invertebrates, sea birds. Listed as being potentially dangerous to man.
Biology:	Viviparous. Up to 140 pups a litter.
Status (IUCN)	Near threatened

GREENLAND SHARK
(Somniosus microcephalus)

Size:	Maximum 7 metres (22 ft 9 ins)
Identification:	Very large shark, heavy body. Grey brown colour.
Distribution:	North Atlantic and Arctic.
Habitat:	Continental and insular shelves to 1200 metres.
Diet/Behaviour:	Fishes, invertebrates, seals, seabirds and scavenges. Slow moving.
Biology:	Ovoviviparous up to 10 pups a litter.
Status (IUCN)	Near threatened

NURSEHOUND SHARK
(Scyliorhinus stellaris)

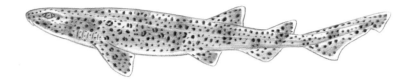

Size: Maximum 1.6 metres (5ft 4 ins)
Identification: Pale golden brown background with black spots.
Distribution: Northeast Atlantic and Mediterranean.
Habitat: Continental and insular shelves to 100 metres.
Diet/Behaviour: Eats crustaceans. Does well in captivity.
Biology: Ovoviviparous. Up to 15 pups a litter.
Status (IUCN)   Near threatened

PORBEAGLE SHARK
(Lamna nasus)

Size: Maximum 3 metres (9 – 10 ft)
Identification: Stout stocky shark. Distinctive white marking on rear of front
                   dorsal fin.
Distribution: Temperate and cool seas, northern and southern hemispheres.
Habitat: Inshore to open ocean.
Diet/Behaviour: Small fishes, small sharks, squid. Migratory and will school.
Biology: Ovoviviparous/oophagy/normally 4 or 5 pups a litter.
Status (IUCN)   Critacally endangered

BLUNTNOSE SIXGILL SHARK
(Hexanchus griseus)

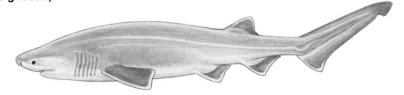

Size:	Maximum 4.82 metres (15 ft 8 ins)
Identification:	Large shark with broad head and wide mouth. Grey to black with a light coloured lateral line.
Distribution:	Worldwide except probably not in the Arctic and Antarctic.
Habitat:	Shelves and slopes of continents, mid ocean ridges and islands.
Diet/Behaviour:	Squid, pelagic bony fishes, small sharks and rays. Large specimens may take small cetaceans and seals. Slow strong swimming shark generally observed as being docile except when captured or in baited situations.
Biology:	Ovoviviparous, large litters of up to 100 pups.
Status (IUCN)	Near threatened

SHARPNOSE SEVENGILL SHARK
(Heptranchias perlo)

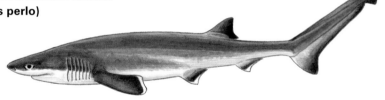

Size:	Maximum 1.4 metres (4 ft 6 ins)
Identification:	Seven pairs of gill slits, pointed head, narrow mouth with large eyes.
Distribution:	Worldwide throughout tropical and temperate seas except the Northeast Pacific.
Habitat:	Occasionally shallow but mostly deepwater
Diet/Behaviour:	Small sharks, squid, pelagic fishes, and crustaceans. Strong swimmer, little known about behaviour.
Biology:	Ovoviviparous, up to 20 pups per litter.
Status (IUCN)	Near threatened

SHORTFIN MAKO SHARK
(Isurus oxyrinchus)

Size:	Maximum 4 metres (13 ft)
Identification:	Blue, purple to black topside, light (whitish) below.
Distribution:	Worldwide in temperate and tropical seas.
Habitat:	Oceanic and coastal. Surface down to 500 – 600 metres.
Diet/Behaviour:	Fishes, squid, smaller sharks maybe small cetaceans.
	Said to be the fastest swimming shark in the world.
Biology:	Ovoviviparous, up to 25 pups a litter.
Status (IUCN)	Vulnerable

SMALLSPOTTED CATSHARK
(Scyliorhinus canicula)

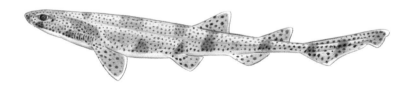

Size:	Maximum 0.45 metres (18 inches)
Identification:	Slender, dark spots on light background.
Distribution:	Northeast Atlantic, North Sea, Mediterranean.
Habitat:	Continental shelves.
Diet/Behaviour:	Small crustaceans, gastropods, cephalopods, fishes. Young
	often in shallower water.
Biology:	Oviparous.
Status (IUCN)	Least concern

STARRY SMOOTHHOUND SHARK
(Mustelus asterias)

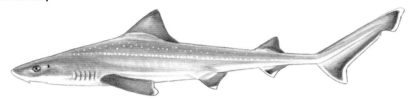

Size:	Maximum 1.4 metres (4 ft 7 ins)
Identification:	Small white spots (stars) on grey brown above, lighter below.
Distribution:	Northeast Atlantic and Mediterranean.
Habitat:	Continental and insular shelves to 100 metres.
Diet/Behaviour:	Eats crustaceans. Does well in captivity.
Biology:	Ovoviviparous. Up to 15 pups a litter.
Status (IUCN)	Least concern

SOUPFIN SHARK (TOPE)
(Galeorhinus galeus)

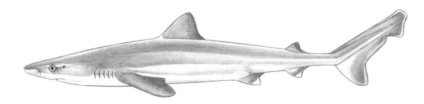

Size:	Maximum 1.64 metres (5 ft 4 ins)
Identification:	Fairly slender. Grey to grey brown above, lighter below, short snout.
Distribution:	Temperate, Mediterranean & northeast Atlantic. Maybe also in South Atlantic.
Habitat:	Continental and insular shelves to 100 metres.
Diet/Behaviour:	Eats bony fishes and invertebrates. Often forms schools.
Biology:	Ovoviviparous. Up to 50 pups a litter.
Status (IUCN)	Vulnerable

SPURDOG SHARK (SPINY DOGFISH)
(Squalus acanthias)

Size:	Maximum 2.0 metres (6 ft 5 ins)
Identification:	Blue grey above, lighter below, sometimes with white spots on sides.
Distribution:	Worldwide except poles and tropics.
Habitat:	From surface to bottom, continental and insular shelves.
Diet/Behaviour:	Smaller sharks and rays, bony fishes, invertebrates.
Biology:	Ovoviviparous, litters up to 30 pups.
Status (IUCN)	Vulnerable

THRESHER SHARK
(Alopias vulpinus)

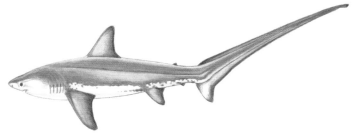

Size:	Maximum 6.10 metres (19 ft 9 ins)
Identification:	Blue to dark grey above, white below.
Distribution:	Worldwide, temperate and tropical seas.
Habitat:	Surface down to 366 metres. Inshore to mid ocean.
Diet/Behaviour:	Bony fishes, squid, small sharks. Known to breach and to hunt co-operatively.
Biology:	Ovoviviparous up to 6 pups a litter.
Status (IUCN)	Vulnerable

RARE AND DEEPWATER SPECIES

ANGULAR ROUGHSHARK
(Oxynotus centrina)

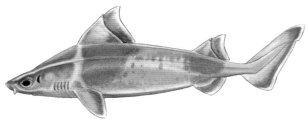

Size: Maximum 1.5 metres (4 ft 9 ins)
Identification: Greyish brown to grey with darker patches.
Distribution: Eastern Atlantic and Mediterranean.
Habitat: Mostly below 100 metres down to 600 metres.
                   Continental shelves.
Diet/Behaviour: Eats worms, molluscs and crustaceans.
                   Little known of behaviour.
Biology: Litters between 7 and 23 pups.
Status (IUCN)   Vulnerable

SAILFIN ROUGHSHARK
(Oxynotus paradoxus)

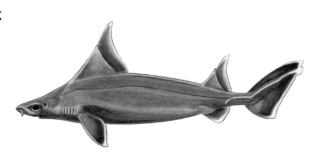

Size: Maximum 1.18 metres (3 ft 9 ins)
Identification: Dark brown/black. Two tall dorsal fins.
Distribution: Northeast Atlantic.
Habitat: Continental slope. Deepwater down to 720 metres.
Diet/Behaviour: Little known.
Biology: Ovoviviparous.
Status (IUCN)   Data deficient

BIRDBEAK DOGFISH
(Deania calcea)

Size:	Maximum 1.22 metres (4 ft)
Identification:	Grey to dark brown, lighter underneath. Very long flat snout.
Distribution:	East Atlantic, Australia, Peru to Chile, New Zealand, Japan.
Habitat:	Deepwater. Continental and insular shelves down to 1500 metres.
Diet/Behaviour:	Bony fishes and shrimps. Sometimes schools.
Biology:	Ovoviviparous. Up to twelve pups per litter.
Status (IUCN)	Least concern

LEAFSCALE GULPER SHARK
(Centrophorus squamosus)

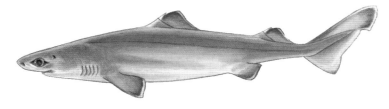

Size:	Maximum 1.6 metres (5 ft 3 ins)
Identification:	Grey brown or reddish brown. Rough skin, flattened snout.
Distribution:	Atlantic and west Pacific and Indian oceans.
Habitat:	Deepwater up to 4000 metres.
Diet/Behaviour:	Little known.
Biology:	Ovoviviparous, up to eight pups per litter.
Status (IUCN)	Vulnerable

BLACK DOGFISH
(Centroscyllium fabricii)

Size: Maximum 1.08 metres (3 ft 5 ins)
Identification: Browny black all over. Large eyes.
Distribution: Temperate Atlantic.
Habitat: Outer continental shelves. Deepwater down to 2000 metres.
Diet/Behaviour: Eats bony fishes, cephalopods and crustaceans.
                   Known to school.
Biology: Ovoviviparous. Up to eight pups a litter.
Status (IUCN)   Least concern

GREAT LANTERN SHARK
(Etmopterus princeps)

Size: Maximum 75 centimetres (2 ft 5 ins)
Identification: Dark brown/black all over.
Distribution: Northwest northeast Atlantic. Maybe in south Atlantic
                   & west Pacific.
Habitat: Deepwater. Continental slopes down to 4500 metres.
Diet/Behaviour: Little known.
Biology: Maybe ovoviviparous.
Status (IUCN)   Data deficient

VELVET BELLY SHARK
(Etmopterus spinax)

Size: Maximum 60 centimetres (2 ft)
Identification: Brownish above, black underneath. Very short gill openings.
Distribution: East Atlantic, Mediterranean.
Habitat: Mostly 200-500 metres.
Diet/Behaviour: Eats small fish, squid, crustaceans.
Biology: Ovoviviparous up to 20 pups a litter.
Status (IUCN)   Least concern

BRAMBLE SHARK
(Echinorhinus brucus)

Size: Maximum 3.10 metres (10 ft)
Identification: Light brown/dark brown with black/red spots on back
                  and sides.
Distribution: Mainly east Atlantic and Mediterranean.
Habitat: Continental and Island shelves, deepwater on or near bottom.
Diet/Behaviour: Small sharks, crustaceans and bony fishes.
                  Behaviour little known.
Biology: Ovoviviparous, probably up to 30 pups per litter
Status (IUCN)   Data deficient

BLACKMOUTH CATSHARK
(Galeus melastomus)

Size: Maximum 0.90 metres (3 ft)
Identification: Distinctive circular spots and blotches, darker brown on
                  lighter background.
Distribution: Northeast Atlantic, Mediterranean.
Habitat: Outer continental shelves down to 1000 metres.
Diet/Behaviour: Bottom invertebrates and lantern fish.
Biology: Oviparous up to 13 eggs.
Status (IUCN)   Least concern

FRILLED SHARK
(Chlamydoselachus anguineus)

Size:	Maximum 196 cm (6 ft 5 ins)
Identification:	Dark brown/brownish black. Eel/snake shaped with flat snakelike head.
Distribution:	Usually deepwater, worldwide, rare.
Habitat:	Mostly deepwater, very occasionally at the surface.
Diet/Behaviour:	Squid and deepwater fish.
Biology:	Ovoviviparous, 6/12 pups per litter.
Status (IUCN)	Near threatened

GHOST CATSHARK
(Apristurus manis)

Size:	Maximum 0.85 metres (2 ft 9 ins)
Identification:	Dark grey to black. Broad nostrils, flat head.
Distribution:	Northwest Atlantic, north and southeast Atlantic.
Habitat:	Continental slopes down to 1700 metres.
Diet/Behaviour:	Little known.
Biology:	Little known.
Status (IUCN)	Least concern

ICELAND CATSHARK
(Apristurus laurussoni)

Size:	Maximum 0.67 metres (2 ft 2 ins)
Identification:	Dark brown. Broad flat head, short snout.
Distribution:	Northwest and Northeast Atlantic
Habitat:	Deepwater down to 2000 metres.
Diet/Behaviour:	Little known.
Biology:	Little known.
Status (IUCN)	Data deficient

WHITE GHOST CATSHARK
(Apristurus aphyodes)

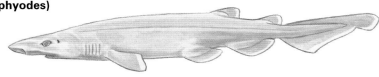

Size:	Maximum 0.54 metres (1 ft 9 ins)
Identification:	Pale whitish grey. Elongated snout.
Distribution:	Northeast Atlantic
Habitat:	Deepwater down to 2000 metres
Diet/Behaviour:	Little known.
Biology:	Little known.
Status (IUCN)	Data deficient

KITEFIN SHARK
(Dalatias licha)

Size:	Maximum 1.82 metres (5 ft 9 ins)
Identification:	Blackish brown all over. Blunt short snout.
Distribution:	Indian, Pacific and Atlantic oceans.
Habitat:	Deepwater to 1800 metres.
Diet/Behaviour:	Deepwater fishes. Lone hunter.
Biology:	Ovoviviparous. Up to 16 pups a litter.
Status (IUCN)	Near threatened

LONGNOSE VELVET DOGFISH
(Centroselachus crepidater)

Size: Maximum 1.05 metres (3 ft 5 ins)
Identification: Long snout. Slender and brown to black in colour.
Distribution: East Atlantic, Indian – Pacific.
Habitat: Mostly 500 metres. Down to 2000 metres.
Diet/Behaviour: Fish and cephalopods.
Biology: Ovoviviparous, up to 8 pups a litter.
Status (IUCN)   Least concern

KNIFETOOTH DOGFISH
(Scymnodon ringens)

Size: Maximum 1.10 metres (3 ft 7 ins)
Identification: Black all over. Short snout.
Distribution: East Atlantic.
Habitat: Deepwater. 200 – 1600 metres.
Diet/Behaviour: Little known.
Biology: Probably ovoviviparous.
Status (IUCN)   Data deficient

VELVET DOGFISH
(Zameus squamulosus)

Size: Maximum 0.69 metres (2 ft 4 ins)
Identification: Black all over. Flat head, long narrow snout.
Distribution: Patchy worldwide except eastern Pacific.
Habitat: Deepwater 500 – 1500 metres, continental and insular shelves.
Diet/Behaviour: Little known.
Biology: Probably ovoviviparous.
Status (IUCN)   Data deficient

PORTUGUESE DOGFISH
(Centroscymnus coelolepis)

Size:	Maximum 1.2 metres (3 ft 10 ins)
Identification:	Black to golden brown. Short snout.
Distribution:	Atlantic, Indian and Pacific oceans.
Habitat:	On or near bottom, mostly 400-500 metres.
Diet/Behaviour:	Other sharks, bony fishes, cetaceans.
Biology:	Ovoviviparous up to 17 pups per litter.
Status (IUCN)	Near threatened

SMOOTH HAMMERHEAD
(Sphyrna zygaena)

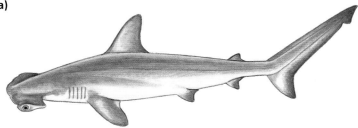

Size:	Maximum 4.0 metres (13 ft)
Identification:	Dark greyish brown above, white below. Large hammerhead.
Distribution:	Worldwide in temperate and tropical waters.
Habitat:	Continental & insular shelves. Mostly near surface.
Diet/Behaviour:	Bony fishes, small sharks, skates & rays.
	Often forms large schools.
Biology:	Viviparous. 30-40 pups per litter.
Status (IUCN)	Vulnerable

THANKS AND ACKNOWLEDGEMENTS

I would like to thank the following either for having provided source material or for their direct personal contribution.

Jane Attwood

Rob Allen

Thomas B Allen – *author* – *The Shark Almanac*

Brian Bates

Chris Bennett – *Porbeagle world record holder (angling)*

Peter Benchley – *author* – *various*

Karl Bennett – *skipper* - *Mantis*

Tony Bennett

Mark Boothman

John Boyle

Michael Bright – *author* – *Private lives of Sharks*

Phill Britts – Skipper – *Blue Fox*

Anthony Bush/Tim Davison – *Editors*

June Bush – *Typing edited manuscripts*

Brigadier J.A.L. Caunter *(Deceased)* – *author* – *Shark Angling at Looe*

Mark Cawardine/Ken Watterson – *authors* – *Shark Watchers Handbook*

Collins – *Sharks of the World*

Marc Dando

Elasmo Films

Chris Fallows

Teresa Farino – *authoress* - *Sharks*

Ian Fergusson

Sarah Fowler

Claudine Gibson (IUCN (SSG)

Richard E. Grant

Dr. Simon Greenstreet

Monty Halls

Philip Harding

Denise Headon – *secretary* – *worn out typing fingers*

Tim Higham

Ali Hood – *The Shark Trust*

Trevor Housby – *author*

Sally Houseago

Martin Kurzik - BBC

Sir David Jason

Miranda Krestovnikoff

Richard Lock

Alex MacCormick – *author* – *Shark Attack*

Marine Conservation Society

Gavin Maxwell – *author* – *Harpoon at a Venture*

Mac McDiarmid – *author* – *Shark Attack*

David Mellor

Stuart Nicholls

John Nightingale

Stuart Patterson

Jacqueline Peirce – *wife* – *incalculable support*

Rowly Pillman

Tony Pimm

Readers Digest – *Sharks*

John Reynolds – *skipper*

Linda Reynolds

Simon Rogerson

Shark Angling Club of Great Britain

Shark Conservation Society

Shark Bay Films

Sally Sharrock

Simon Spear

Colin Speedie

Jeremy Stafford-Deitsch

Darren Steadwood

The Shark Trust

Jed Trewin

David Turner

Paul Vincent

Danny Vokins

Jim Watson

Ken Watterson

Chris Wylie – *Cartoonist*

and anyone I have forgotten.

ABOUT THE AUTHOR

I have been lucky enough to have had a long and 'glittering career' with more ups and downs than a 90-year-old getting the birthday bumps, and certainly comprising as many downs as ups! My education in Cornwall and then Devon came to an abrupt end when I left school in the middle of a sixth form term to join a rock and roll band and become a megastar. However, as starvation was more of a possibility than stardom, I decided to move into managing rock bands and capped this part of my career by making the "brilliant" decision to turn down a singer who went on to have a huge hit that for many years held the record of being the longest running British Number One. In fact, so good was my rock and roll judgement that, together with Paul Gardner and Terry Sullivan of Rainbow Reflection, I also made the "clever" decision not to follow up on an opportunity to work with David Bowie – a year later he was a superstar. Our time in horseracing was marked by a similar discerning decision. My wife and I decided we couldn't afford to buy a yearling colt for £5,000 which went on to earn over £1,000,000 for its owner.

The Peirces have a long "East of Suez" history. My great-grandfather started Peirce Leslie & Co. in 1862, which became one of South India's leading companies. My uncle and cousin followed in his footsteps and also had distinguished careers in the Subcontinent. After spending time as a "guest" of the Japanese on the river Kwai in World War Two, my father spent most of his Army career in the Middle East, where I, too, have spent a large part of my life. This has given me a love of the desert, and an appreciation of the political history and tensions in the region that have so sadly contributed to the terrorism currently plaguing the world. I returned to the UK in the late 1980s, but up until that time had spent more of my life in Arabia than Britain. I have continued to travel regularly to the region and, at the time of writing, have carried out shark research expeditions in Kuwait and Qatar, and have expeditions in Bahrain, Lebanon, Egypt and Yemen in various stages of planning.

Sharks were one of my childhood obsessions and never seem to have been far away. I have early memories of being warned to be careful of sharks when growing up in Egypt, and of a possibly fatal attack in Kuwait when I was 8 or 9. My mother gave me a Jacques Cousteau shark book when I was in my early teens, and in the Red Sea, Arabian Sea, Arabian Gulf and Indian Ocean, I have been lucky enough to encounter sharks throughout my life.

In more recent years I re-started the tag-and-release programme with the Shark Angling Club in Looe, became a member of the mainland board of the Basking Shark Society, and joined the Shark Trust in 1999, later becoming a Trustee and then Chairman. In the late 1990's I started the Richard Peirce Shark Conservation Fund which morphed into the Shark Conservation Society in 2008. In 2002 I began running research trips and expeditions, and in 2006 I started the first cage diving in the UK. Over the past eighteen years or so, I have been giving shark talks all over Britain, and at the time of writing am working on my fifth shark book.

I have earned a living variously in journalism, the music business, advertising, public relations, marketing, acting, capital and defence equipment sales, consultancy, farming, running a restaurant, retailing, and breeding racehorses. I suppose this makes me a jack of many trades but I hope a master of one or two of them. After selling our stud farm in Buckinghamshire in 1999, my wife and I moved back to Cornwall, largely so that I would have more time to devote to various shark activities. Since the first edition of Sharks in British Seas was published in 2008 shark conservation has come a long way, however there is still much work to be done if extinctions are to be averted.

Close personal proximity to and contact with wars in the Middle East, various land predators, sharks, copulating stallions and mares, rock and roll, armies and weapons, politicians, my earlier headstrong nature, and my having lost my father, brother and mother, have left me mildly surprised that I am still alive. I have a wonderful wife, two fabulous daughters and a large family. So far its been a great ride, most of the time......